AND I WAS LIKE
NOVEMBER

© Copyright 2023 - All rights reserved.

The content contained within this book may not be reproduced, duplicated or transmitted without direct written permission from the author or the publisher.

Under no circumstances will any blame or legal responsibility be held against the publisher, or author, for any damages, reparation, or monetary loss due to the information contained within this book, either directly or indirectly.

Legal Notice:

This book is copyright protected. It is only for personal use. You cannot amend, distribute, sell, use, quote or paraphrase any part, or the content within this book, without the consent of the author or publisher.

For Andrew,
    Because a terrible person is an excellent muse.

AND I WAS LIKE NOVEMBER

Baby on Board 9

Twelve-teen 23

Seven Days of Weak 49

Illustrious Longing 69

Rainbows and Lollipops 79

Burning 89

Peg and Pete's Precarious Predicament 93

Cyanide Soup 111

Feral Femme 125

A Helping Hand 137

Eleven Days 'til Sunday 155

Madonna Whore 175

One Thousand Dollars 179

Uzair and the Bear 199

And I Was Like November 215

Baby on Board

Deliberately inhaling and exhaling the crisp morning air with force, Jane noticed one of the first leaves turning yellow and felt grateful that Autumn was not far off and the tourists would soon depart with their I love NY T-shirts and dozens of pictures of signature landmarks that no one cared to look at.

She jogged by two women with strollers that were engulfed in conversation, probably about breastfeeding and stretch marks and baby's first solid food. She smiled wanly, but without a baby, she was invisible to them. She consoled herself by turning around to look at their widened hips and sensible handbags full of bottles, wash cloths and whatever other nonsense they dutifully packed around. Aiming to beat her best time of six minutes around the perimeter of the park today, she left the matrons in her dust.

Sweaty and content she stopped for a seven-dollar latte and a leisurely read through the Sunday Times before arriving home to find a hand-made invitation to her cousin Sarah's wedding shower waiting in the mailbox. "Fuck," she whispered, as Bethany, her eighty-something landlady looked up from her mail with an understanding smirk.

"Bad news?"

"My cousin's shower."

"Is it leaking?" she laughed at her own joke.

"Worse. Another wedding."

"You don't like weddings?"

"I'm sick of pretending to care about another inane measurement of where we're supposed to be and what we're supposed to be doing designed to keep us brain dead because we're too busy picking out cakes to care about what's really going on."

"Are you angry about something, honey?"

Jane stepped down from her soap box.

"I beat my best time around the park today."

"Now, *that's* an accomplishment!"

"Thanks."

"Don't compare yourself to those people. One day they will have hit all the milestones they're told they're supposed to and there will be nothing left to strive for and even if there were, there wouldn't be time between the hungry mouths and the baseball games. It's the striving that makes us happy you know."

"By next weekend I'm going to get my time down to five and a half minutes."

"There used to be no choice for women. You were a spinster or a homosexual or just pitifully unfortunate if you didn't have children."

Jane could feel the likelihood of getting stuck talking to Bethany for another forty minutes increase with every word. She felt simultaneously guilty and fearful that one day she would be the old woman hanging around the mailboxes desperate for conversation.

"I know and I'm sorry you had to live through that. I've got to clean up. I've got a lunch date."

She turned and started up the stairs smiling and waving, so as not to be rude.

"Have fun, darling," Bethany called after her.

Once inside her apartment, Jane made herself a smoothie full of all the right things to keep her looking twenty-five until she was forty-five and sat on the floor with her back against the couch. She opened her computer and went to the dreaded social media sites created for an occasion just such as this, when an otherwise sane woman wanted to compare herself to others in order to perpetuate self-loathing.

She looked at her cousin's page. There it was. The ring and the hashtags and the guy whose primary role was to secure her cousin's status as marriage-worthy. Jane remembered the days of buying her booze underage and hearing the stories of the losers she'd slept with when she blacked-out. This future husband of hers would never know that though. He would never hear the stories of blow jobs in bathroom stalls or tree sap in her hair from when she used to take suitors behind the portable in tenth grade. She was wife material now and her shiny ring proved it.

The following weekend Jane got her time down to 5 minutes and 46 seconds and though it wasn't the five and a half she had hoped, it kept her striving.

She'd been out for dinner and a little too much wine last night with a co-worker's brother and she felt it. The guy was partner at a prestigious law firm with a ski condo and a yoga habit at some passé studio everyone had heard of. No one told him that being six-feet-tall and able to buy material goods wasn't meant to substitute for a personality.

Jane was at the point in her life where dating struggling musicians or bartenders with coke habits was frowned upon though. She saw the judgement when she chose interesting men over secure ones. Her cousin's wedding would be a melee of queries about why she wasn't married or at the very least seriously involved. Did she even have a beau? they'd ask. Did she not want a *family*?

The truth was she didn't know. It seemed like a nice idea. It sounded so easy to know that instead of being the oddball single, you could invite everyone to your suburban house for dinner by way of a Christmas card with a photo of some kids that resembled you or the other adult in the photo, save for a few missing teeth and unmanageable cowlicks. She fantasized about the photos she could post of her honeymoon in at an all-inclusive in the Cays or Cancun, as if this husband figure of hers would be enough to anesthetize her to the predictability of buffets and umbrella drinks.

And then there would be the babies. Would she get a minivan? Oh, hell no. But who's to say? Did her cousin think when she was throwing up a mouthful of some stranger's semen that she would someday be baring a *Baby on Board* decal as if adult lives were somehow inferior? Never say never.

The following Sunday, Jane not only made her time, she beat it. Five minutes and 24 seconds. Smiling proudly, she sat on a bench to catch her breath. Beside her, a woman with a fancy stroller filled with a fancy baby prattled on her phone about getting in shape whilst slurping a 700-calorie frozen coffee drink. She was focused on the jungle gym off in the distance, presumably at another of her spawn and didn't seem to notice sweaty Jane. The fancy baby did though. She watched Jane's every move until she made eye-contact and joyfully returned the smile Jane still wore from beating her best time. The smiling baby was a girl, as evidenced by her decadent pink down coat complete with ears. Though she wasn't sure what kind of animal had pink ears, maybe a pig, Jane was charmed in spite of herself.

She did her best to look stoic, but the happy girl-child was having none of it. She continued to smile and gaze at Jane with impish eyes that sparkled like the pond they sat beside. When she began to blow bubbles with her tiny bowed lips and wave her chubby little hands, Jane melted. Before long the twosome was engaged in passionate flirtation, neither able to get enough of the other.

A moment later, there was a scream in the distance, followed by a burst of dramatic tears and the presumed mother of this adorably gleeful baby tore herself off the bench and dashed toward the playground.

Jane didn't pay much attention at first, smitten as she was with the baby who was now outright laughing at their game of peek-a-boo. It was quite possibly the sweetest sound in the world—like cherubic harps strumming, and clouds opening up to allow sunlight to beam solely on Jane. She felt overwhelmed with love for this child who just moments ago she hadn't even known. Was this how it was for soul mates? Was this the love at first site she'd heard so many basic bitches babble about?

If this baby was hers, there's no way in hell she would run away and leave her alone. Was it possible her mother didn't want this gleaming little angel? Maybe the kid she'd run after was her favorite and she was she fed up with shitty diapers and someone hanging off her nipple.

She thought about stories of babies being left on doorstops, or nowadays at fire stations, and wondered if this was a fate such as that. She'd seen the bumper stickers on police cars and ambulances that said, 'Don't Abandon Your Baby' and wondered if seeing that in writing was enough to deter people who might actually be considering it. Jane's face turned somber and the baby mimicked with concerned empathy. The connection with this child was undeniable.

The mother was well out of site now. Was this her cue? She looked around. No one was watching. If anyone were, they would assume Jane was the mother and having just finished a jog around the park, was heading home to her husband where he'd spend the day doing home improvements and she preparing a nutritious meal between laundry and a trip to Pottery Barn.

She imagined her real life with this baby. The rapture of waking up to her smile. Her first steps. The whimsical bedtime stories. The companionship. The sense of purpose and the relief to get out of her head and focus on someone else's well-being was all that was missing from her life. Selflessness was what it was all about, right? *This* was the enlightenment the single ladies sought in their Kundalini and meditation classes.

She would tell people that she had adopted and that she'd wanted it to be a surprise.

She'd come back from maternity leave glowing and force the photos on people that had been forced on her. They'd have to listen to her meaningless chatter about plain things the child had said or done that were truly remarkable to her. She would read the blogs on how to parent and be part of the complaining mom's club. Heck, maybe a mini-van would be a practical mode of transportation once the girl became school-aged and carpool was needed for all of her friends to get to dance practice and sleepovers in the suburbs.

She stroked the baby's downy hair and the little one yawned.

"Ohhh, are you tired honey-bear? Do you want to come home with me and have a snuggle?"

She stared longer at this gorgeous little nugget. Her innocence brought tears to Jane's eyes.

"I'm going to take such good care of you. We're going to be so happy together, you and I. We're going to have to give you a name, aren't we? Helena? Madeline? How about Harper? I've always liked Harper for a girl."

She looked toward the playground. She could see the woman that had been sitting beside her. She was wiping the nose of a four-year-old boy on her sleeve and talking gently to him, still with no mind of the baby she'd left alone.

Jane stood, planning the quickest route home in her mind. If anyone caught her, she'd say she ran up and found the abandoned infant and was riddled with concern. She was going to take her to the nearest police station.

Why not call 911? the authorities might ask. Because she never brought her phone on runs. It was a much-needed technology break.

The baby's eyes were closing intermittently, on the brink of sleep where she might dream of lilies and doves and halos woven of baby's breath, but then out of nowhere, she coughed, her little lungs needing to rid themselves of something impure. Jane's plans to kidnap her perhaps.

The mother's ears perked up like a German Shepard hearing his master's car turn onto their street and she scooped her son up and started over in their direction. Jane picked up the coughing baby, knowing as fast as she was, she could get away on foot before the mother could give a decent eye-witness account, but along with the weight of the child in her arms, she felt the weight of being a mother beyond the first steps, whimsical bedtime stories and morning smiles when the baby sneezed forcefully, expelling an ungodly amount of green snot onto Jane's cheek and into her hair. Horrified, Jane did her best not to scream and drop the baby. She succeeded, but the fantasy came to a screeching halt.

What if she wasn't cut out for wiping noses with her sleeve, interrupted sleep and making endless chicken nuggets or macaroni and cheese? She didn't feel confident that she wouldn't be tempted to eat these foods if they were in the house for this child, and then what? Her body would go to shit, hell, he whole life could go to shit! And so when the baby's haggard mother appeared, Jane handed over the child who had since stopped coughing and was back to her delightful disposition, playfully tapping Jane's snot-soaked face.

"Oh, thank you so much for watching Daisy! My 'adventurous' son," she laughed at her own air quotes, "had a spill and I could tell you were trustworthy. You're so good with her; you must be mom."

"I didn't realize you'd seen me."

"We see everything, don't we?"

"Right. Mom's see it all."

"Do you have a picture of your kids?"

"No, I left my phone at home. Needed a technology break."

Jane untangled her hair from the baby's fist and handed her over.

"Gotta get back to my little ones. My husband's re-tiling our downstairs bathroom today."

And with that, she sprung like a gazelle and made it home in her best time yet.

Twelve-teen

Beaver Point Hall was a wooden A-frame with peeling white paint and a blue trim reminiscent of a time long gone, but here we were in 1988. It sat at the edge of the woods near the end of an endlessly long country road and shared its rocky driveway with a red preschool where actual preschoolers went to sing songs and grow string beans. Rachel and I climbed through the window without checking the door, which was probably open. We were best, *best* friends and felt fated from the moment we met with much in common. Besides having the same name, we both arrived for grade seven at Saltspring Elementary from broken homes, mine with more scandal, but neither of us lived behind a white picket fence. Born two weeks apart, we were Leos, something we took very seriously, cutting out and sharing every horoscope we saw and making them mean what we hoped they did. We sprayed our teased bangs with so much hairspray, gravity wondered why it bothered to exist and our make-up was an array of so many contrasting colors it made our neon slouch socks look neutral. Being so similar to someone was justification for everything we did. When in doubt, do what the other one would.

There were some minor distinctions. She was a redhead, I wasn't. She had a sister, I didn't. The big one though, was that she put effort into her schoolwork, so wasn't failing every subject and getting grief about it from principals and vice principals, which was such a drag. Around report cards I always hated her a little. I got more attention from boys though, which made her hate *me* a lot.

We'd given ourselves two hours to hitch a ride from the opposite end of the island since it was easier to sneak in if we got there before Hilda the door hippy was collecting admission, but we got picked up after walking only twenty minutes, and now here we were. Very early.

We got high and played with the Playdough at the schoolhouse. I made a caterpillar by rolling up balls of each color and sticking them together. I poked eyes in its skull with a pencil crayon as Rachel stuck her hand in a tray of paint and left her print on the wall. I joined her when I finished my caterpillar, reveling in the cool wet texture and how small my blue handprint looked on the white wall compared to how important it felt.

I resented that I couldn't take more pot from my dad's stash, but my simple-minded stepmom, Daphne caught me with my hand in the baggie the previous week and giggled with menace as though she would hold this chance to blackmail me over my head forever.

My dad didn't care if I smoked weed, as long as it wasn't *his* weed since he was always stressing over money. If I left a light on when I went out of the room for 20 seconds, he told me I should get a job and pay the electric bill for a change and if there was a school trip, I wasn't going unless Grandma coughed up fifty bucks. Some mornings he left me the change in his jeans to buy fries and gravy for lunch and some mornings he didn't. Maybe he was grumpy from too many beers the night before, or he'd gotten another call from the damned school, or maybe he just didn't have any spare change.

It was 9 o' clock before a car engine interrupted the quiet humming that might only have been inside my head. The poster said eight, but that was a ballpark for Rastafarian musicians. Washing up, our giggling gained momentum when the bar of soap slipped out of my hands and by the time we made our way down to the hall we were back to our usual hysterics.

We crouched in the bushes watching the darkest-skinned men we'd ever seen unload their equipment, snickering quietly at their African attire because we were a world of two and everyone was fodder for our ridicule.

When the coast was clear we went in the side door and through the kitchen where Sally Sunshine was pulling a cookie sheet out of the oven, her unruly grey hair perched atop her head with a chopstick poking through.

"Hey girls! Wanna samosa?" she asked, shining her toothy yellow grin.

Was her sunshine moniker because of the golden teeth? I wondered, hoping I'd remember to share this hilarious possibility later.

"Sure!" Rachel said reaching for a curry-smelling triangle.

I had no idea what they were, but any kind of food sounded amazing as spittle gathered at the corners of my mouth.

We hung out with Sally for a bit and drank the sulphury tap water while she bustled around getting ready to sell her wares. A few people trickled in as dusk descended. Kids jumped around and rolled over each other on the dance floor like piles of puppies. It looked like a good time, but a different kind than I was allowed to have anymore.

The night got rockin' and the hall was packed. It was worth the wait as the music got inside me and made nothing else matter. Patchouli oil, sweat and a heavy cloud of pot smoke wafted through the air as we swayed in our pre-pubescent bodies, their awkwardness vastly magnified by a high that was mostly just a dull headache and a hefty dose of self-consciousness now.

On the edge of the dance floor, I saw Dominic, his strawberry blonde hair hanging over one eye with his freakishly skinny buddy, Sun. Dominic's clothes seemed modern and stylish cuz he'd been living in a suburb of Toronto before coming to our shitty little island. He was exotic. His parents came before him while he was detained as a juvenile delinquent for breaking into cars. I met him here, at Beaver Point Hall, and when we couldn't get a ride home, he, Rachel and I had slept on the same kitchen floor we'd just had samosas on. He put his finger inside me and his tongue so far down my throat I nearly gagged and neither of those things had happened before, so I guessed it meant we were bonded for eternity. I only saw him three more times before he dumped me for Sky, probably because she had boobs already. One of my nipples was starting to swell, but it couldn't be called a boob. Someday.

I waved at Dominic and he gave me a nod. When I looked back a minute or two later, he was talking to a native guy with shoulder length black hair and a black and grey varsity jacket. Dominic waved us over. I tapped Rachel on the shoulder. "Dominic's here!"

"Maybe he has pot!" Her eyes widened hopefully.

We made our way through the tie-dye, dreadlocks and crocheted beanies, past the bare feet, ankle bracelets and hairy armpits to Dominic, Sun and the native guy with the varsity jacket who was called an Indian back then in a way that wasn't racist or incorrect, it just was.

"Meet me at the truck," I heard him say gruffly to Dominic.

"You guys wanna smoke?" Dominic yelled over the drum beat.

Rachel and I nodded enthusiastically and followed them up the hill to the native guy's truck.

Dominic opened the door to get in the front seat but the native guy stopped him. "Let one of the girls sit up here."

We couldn't decide who, so we both hopped in and since we only weighed 80 pounds each, cramming our bony butts into one seat was fine. Staying close to each other was more important than comfort anyway.

Sitting down felt tremendous and the quiet was a blanket of relief.

"I'm Lorne," said the native guy.

"I'm Rachel," said Rachel.

"And I'm Rachael too," I said, and we both burst into giggles.

"Alright, double trouble!" said Lorne and we all laughed again like it was the funniest thing anyone had ever said. "How old are ya?"

We looked at each other wondering if we should lie. Rachel spoke first. "Twelve," she said.

I elbowed her in the ribs. "I'll be thirteen in July," hoping she hadn't blown our chance to sit in this nice warm truck.

"Right on, man. Girls over sixteen aren't any fun."

Phewf.

"How old are you?" I asked.

"I'm 39," he said, laughing loudly as he threw his head back like a wolf howling at the moon and then without taking a breath, said with absolute seriousness, "Let's get stoned."

"Yeah!" we said in unison laughing at that with the guys joining in. I liked feeling funny, and the right age, and that life was a big party.

Twelve-teen

We sat there for an hour smoking and giggling, listening to Pink Floyd and Led Zeppelin. We knew Stairway to Heaven from the radio, so we played it on repeat and sang along. Lorne was really fun and didn't seem like an adult at all except that he had so much weed and the nice warm car.

"You guys thirsty?" he asked.

"I am *so thirsty!*"

"Oh my God, my mouth is a desert."

"It's like I'm a camel and I haven't seen water for six days." I moved my neck how I thought a camel might and Rachel joined in.

We all laughed some more until Lorne spoke gruffly to Dominic. "Get the cooler bag."

Dominic handed a blue foil bag to us.

"Feel how crinkly this is!" I said, and Rachel and I took turns crunching the texture between our fingers.

"Can I get a pop?" Sun asked.

"No pop, that shit'll rot your brains."

"Here girls, hand Sun a drink."

There were so many exotic choices. Guava juice, a pineapple coconut blend and a lime spritz. I handed Sun

31.

a cloudy guava juice and after much deliberation, chose a can of Mango Fandango for myself. Its deliciousness was mind bending. Lorne pulled out a bag of smoked almonds from under his seat and Rachel and I devoured them like hungry rats. He seemed to want to make us happy and it was totally working. We didn't go back inside the dancehall, instead he drove us home, even taking me all the way up my stupidly long driveway. I felt like a princess until I ran into my dad.

"Who the fuck was that?!" he shouted from the top of the stairs where he stood in his underwear and the thin blue robe he'd thrown on without tying the belt.

"Rachel's mom."

"Yeah, right." He grunted and turned.

"Night, dad," I said in a wobbly voice.

About a week later, Rachel and I were walking home from school laughing and plotting our weekend, wondering where the party would be and who we could get to buy our liquor when we heard a car coming. It was rare for car to be this far out of town. My white Keds were soaked grey with rain water and I crossed my fingers making a wish that this car would pick us up. We were fortunate to live on the same windy country road about ten minutes apart, but miles from anywhere else. Mine was a four-bedroom rental house on four acres. The heading in the classified ad my stepmom circled said 4 on four, which was clever, I guess. When I wanted to get out of the house and had nowhere to go, I'd walk to the pond and listen to the frogs. I could never *ever* see one, as hard as I looked, but they yelled and screamed as loud as my boredom.

Rachel's mother and stepdad were icy British nudists who ran a bed and breakfast, so it made sense for them to live so far out of town; mine just wanted to torture me I guess. Tourists found the remoteness charming and idyllic. Idiots. When I'd stay over, it was normal to run into one of her parents in the hallway and nearly die of embarrassment at the sight of her mom's boobs hanging at different lengths or her stepdad's nub of a penis poking out from his full bush.

I turned around first to see if I recognized the car, and praise God, I did.

"Yessss! It's Lorne!"

"Oh my God, sweet!"

We both waved enthusiastically and he pulled over.

"Hey, hey, pretty ladies. Hop in!"

"Hiiii!"

"Hurry up, so no one sees you," he said in a more serious tone. I guessed because we had smoked so much pot with him and that was illegal.

We started hanging out with Lorne a lot after that. We'd sit in the park in the middle of town with absolutely nothing to do after school and he'd drive through like a knight coming to rescue us from watching more damned hacky sacking. He'd take us to the convenience store and give us each twenty buck-a-roos, while he waited in the alley behind, his truck idling. We got the expensive ice cream bars, chips, chocolate and penny candies. One day Rachel even got chip dip like we were some kind of millionaires.

Mr. Lam, the store's owner, never spoke to us. He just rang everything in, happy to have the business, glad it wasn't his goody-two-shoes daughter eating all this junk.

We'd go for drives with Lorne, delighted to be dry, with free pot, listening to tunes and snacking. It was the height of luxury. Previously we might get picked up by teenaged boys that tried to shove their hands down our tight jeans while driving their junky cars recklessly and smashing mailboxes with baseball bats, which didn't titillate me at all.

We got nicknamed twelve-teens by one of the obnoxious 17-year-olds with a muffler-free Pinto and I guess that made us seem closer in age for an attempted finger bang in this strange, lawless town.

A couple of girls had cars, but they didn't want to hang out with us given the social hierarchy. Twelve-year-olds weren't cool, except to Lorne. He was like a kindly uncle we could do no wrong in front of. He was an audience for our antics and said yes to any of our requests. He talked to us about the perils of alcohol, how important it was to be creative, and said that police were the real bad guys. When I said that I wanted to marry a businessman (because on television they represented success and everything that this island wasn't), he passionately objected saying that they were the most corrupt and abusive men on earth and that I should stick with artists because they respected women.

Lorne was a sculptor whose pieces sold in galleries across Canada. He had a dusty studio in the garage at his house five minutes from town and one day he took us there to show us his carvings. Rachel was more interested than me but when she went to the bathroom, he showed me a hunk of rock and said it would be my wedding gift when he married me, and I was flattered even though I didn't want to be.

When Rachel came out, I cornered her, "Oh my God, you'll never guess what Lorne said to me!"

"What?!"

"He said he wanted to marry me one day and he was like making me a carving for our wedding."

"Oh yeah, he hits on me all the time, too."

"He does?"

"Yeah, it's like so gross."

"Oh my God, yeah, that's so gross!" I pretended to gag but felt a little mad at her. Was she lying? I was the pretty one. She had so many freckles! She was probably telling a big, fat, jealous lie.

"So like, what did he say?" I asked pretending not to care too much.

"Oh, he's just always like 'you're so pretty' and stuff."

Pfft. Whatever. He said he wanted to marry me. It was totally gross, but marriage meant someone actually loved you and it was better than just being pretty. She was so immature sometimes. Too young to know the meaning of a paradox, I tried not to like it. Just like the other stuff.

On a Wednesday afternoon, with a persistent drizzle hitting my forehead, Lorne and I walked ahead of Rachel, Dominic and Sun toward the truck. I wanted the front seat. Lorne said Rachel and I couldn't share it anymore because it gave the cops a reason to pull us over. I didn't think it mattered much since he always told us to duck down if we saw them, but it wasn't open for debate.

Sun was lost in space, as usual and I could hear Rachel flirting with Dominic again. She said she didn't like him, but the lilt of her voice gave it away.

"Let's go," Lorne said. He used the voice that was usually reserved for bossing Dominic around and I sped up. The truck was parked by the barn around the corner and when we got there, he grabbed my butt and pulled me close to him. I heard myself squeak in an unfamiliar way, but he shoved his tongue between my lips before I could self-deprecate. His stubble scratched my chin and I thought of my grandpa chasing my cousin and I around threatening to give us whisker burns, but this wasn't like that. It wasn't a joke. I could hear the other three getting closer and was terrified they'd see us, but then he stuck his hand down the front of my pants and I forgot to be terrified for about six seconds because he touched a spot that made me feel really, really good. Then Rachel was there and the indignity of reality struck me like a cannonball to the gut. He pulled his hand out and laughed.

"Get up front," he said quietly to me, which was all I wanted to begin with.

Rachel looked at me and raised her eyebrows. Her mouth opened a little, like a marionette. A judgmental marionette that I would have a really hard time explaining this to. Shit.

I sat quietly, staring out the window so that no one would make eye contact. My cheeks were burning and I opened the window, but Lorne protested. "You're letting all the smoke out, baby."

Oh, please don't call me baby in front of them. Please just drop me off at the beach so I can dig a hole in the sand to crawl into until the tide washes me away.

Thank God, my house was first when he drove us home.

"Don't drive up." I mumbled.

"I know, I know," he said.

He let me off where the bus did instead and I walked, my jeans a little damp in the crotch, a regrettable reminder of myself.

I told Rachel the next morning on the bus that I hadn't wanted him to do that. That it was disgusting and that I was never going over there again. I told her that I thought she was right behind me and that she was a bad friend for leaving me alone with him but she just glared at me, so I pulled my trump card.

"You're getting to be pretty good friends with Dom, hey?"

"No. Why? You still like him?" she looked guilty and I knew she'd stop being a bitch.

"I dunno." I looked down at my dirty shoes that I resented so much before now and felt like they were a-okay.

By lunch time we were laughing again, but when the bell rang, I got on the bus without going by her locker like usual. We didn't have plans, but it was unspoken that we would go sit in the park before hitching home. Not today though.

I sat on my bed and stared at the blue carpet. It might've been interesting if I were stoned, but I wasn't, and it was too cold to go commiserate with the frogs.

My dad was working night shift; he wouldn't be home 'til midnight and Daphne was watching her soaps. I went to the kitchen and put some tater tots in the microwave. She was on the phone. Probably to her mom, as usual. Hogging the phone and the TV like the stupid hog she was.

The next weekend there was a party at the beach. Lorne had been giving us money to tidy up his filthy house and the freedom of cash was joyous. He'd hate it if he knew we were buying booze with it, but Rachel and I each got a 26er of rum. Me dark and her light because we were the same, but different. We each got a can of Coke too, which was definitely not enough mix, but it got the first couple of drinks down and then the taste didn't matter. I poured some of mine out to put the rum in and then more and more until it was just a can of rum, which was totally gross, but it barely mattered.

Johnny with the white pick-up bought our booze *and* gave us a ride to the party, which was full of rednecks with their muscle cars and beer bellies. They were the people the tourists never saw. They didn't hang out at coffee shops or the Farmer's Market, and they didn't kayak or go on cycling tours of the art galleries. They drank and fought and raced their souped-up cars, which they talked incessantly about. Their girlfriends wore their denim jackets with the corduroy collars and smoked stubby cigarettes they dug out of their enormous leather purses with the tassels. They wouldn't be caught dead at Beaver Point Hall, but we skated between the two worlds. Twelve-teens who didn't yet know where they fit.

I got so drunk that night I nearly fell into the seven-foot bonfire that the boys had been squirting lighter fluid on between drinking contests and wrestling. I leaned into someone tall as he held out his arms for me, and in a blur I was in the bush with him as he penetrated me, the smell of tree sap inches from my nose. It didn't feel like anything until the next day when my girl parts were on fire. Rachel was bitter that I'd lost my virginity before her and I felt like I was the winner at becoming an adult first.

I started hanging out with Charlotte after that. She'd failed a grade *and* started school late, so she was older—what I wanted to be. Her mom let Charlotte's boyfriend live with them and they'd been having sex for a while. I was in this club now.

Soon after I turned thirteen, Daphne got pregnant. A social worker came and took me to a foster home because she said I'd kicked her in her fat stomach. It wasn't true, but no one believes a thirteen-year-old. I left the foster home after a week and snuck on the ferry back to the island. I went right to Lorne's doorstep at 4pm that afternoon, as though maybe I'd been at school all day and not on the lam. Not that he would've cared.

"Baby! Get in here! Dominic told me what happened." He wrapped his soft familiar arms around me. I exhaled.

We sat on the maroon futon with its rips and stains and he moved closer as we smoked joint after joint. He unzipped his pants and put my hand there. It was hard like the coffee mug leaving a dirty rim on the table but the skin was softer than any I'd ever felt.

"I have to go the bathroom" I said, jumping up. I stayed in there until I heard his sculpting tools buzzing and then crept out and tucked myself under a smoky blanket. I dreamt of eating sawdust because my mouth was so fucking dry.

I got up with the sun in the morning. The air was thick and stale with smoke and there was only ice cream to eat. I wanted an apple or scrambled eggs; something nourishing that wasn't here. I turned the brass doorknob and heard him call out. "Where are you going?"

"I dunno," I mumbled. "Somewhere, I guess."

He gave me a fifty-dollar bill and ten hits of acid wrapped in tin foil. He kissed me hard on the lips. I was so happy to have cash and drugs that I didn't resist.

"Come back later on. I'll be here."

I ran into some friends and we took all of the acid and swam in the lake even though it was October. My teeth chattered and I found the sound entertaining.

My dad let me come home a few days later. That Spring he announced that work had transferred him to somewhere I'd never been and we moved there.

I fumbled through my teenage sexual relationships fast and dirty, to disconnect from the vulnerability I never wanted to feel again. I didn't have a high school sweetheart or a prom date or anything wholesome. I looked fine on the outside, but the filth of my history coursed furiously through my veins making me ugly. I felt like everyone could see what Rachel saw and that she'd told every person I'd ever met or ever would meet long after we stopped knowing each other.

At twenty, I became a stripper and grew skilled at using my body as a tool to get things from men. I had plenty of sex, but enjoyed very little of it. Maybe because

Twelve-teen

I chose men who didn't care if I did, or maybe it reminded me of my mortification that day by Lorne's truck and all the subsequent times, even if it was way deep down.

I didn't think about Lorne or his influence on me until Thanksgiving twenty years later with a friend's family. On their mantle was one his carvings. "Lorne Fineday," I said loudly, as my child and adult world collided and he straddled both.

"You're a fan?" asked my friend's father.

"No," I said flatly. I used to know him. A long time ago."

"Did you know him well?"

"Too well. What about you?"

"I used to run a gallery he showed at. What a talented guy. He led an amazing life. Overcame so much. Did he tell you about being put in residential school at six?"

"He called it boarding school. Said he hated it."

"Oh, they were awful. They did all kinds of just, horrific, I mean really terrible, stuff to these kids."

He paused to see if I wanted to hear. I did.

45.

He lowered his voice and stepped slightly away from his boisterous family. I leaned in. "I mean the nuns and the priests, they were just awful."

"Violence and molesting and stuff?" If it was worse than what Lorne did to me maybe I'd feel vindication.

His eyes widened and he exhaled loudly. "They used to bleach their skin to try and make them more white like us. They'd feed them rotten food and when they threw it up, they'd make them eat that."

Now my eyes widened.

"They raped his cousin and made her have the baby and then bury it by the river. Still alive. Worse things than you can imagine."

My friend's father's lovely wife called out in her German accent, "Who wants to try Kruegel? Christmas Kruegel?" She came over to where we were standing with brightly colored napkins. "What are you two whispering about over here? she asked innocently.

He put his arm around her shoulder and pulled her close. "Rachael used to know Lorne Fineday."

"Ohhh, did you? We were so sorry to lose such a talent. The world has one less genius."

"He died?"

"You didn't know? I'm sorry. It was quite a while ago now. What year would that have been?"

He thought about it. "Well we closed the gallery in 2003?"

"2004," she said surely.

"Right, 2004 and it was about a year after that." He turned to me. "We hadn't spoken to him in a while, but his art wasn't selling like it did and we heard he started drinking again."

"Really? he hated booze."

"Hated it."

"Oh, yeah, didn't touch the stuff for years."

We were quiet for just long enough.

"Kruegel?"

"Sure, yeah, please."

"Thank you my love, I'll give you a hand."

I went down the carpeted stairs taking care to step over the one that creaked on the way in and let myself out.

Seven Days of Weak

Monday

Traditionally the day most people choose to commit suicide and also to die of natural causes, Mondays get a bad rap but they aren't my most unfavorite day. I have caught up on my sleep over the weekend and look forward to putting on make-up and stockings and being re-united with him.

Upon arrival at the bus stop I spot a smattering of vomit. I hold my breath and try not to look, but like any good rebel when I'm not supposed to do something it makes it all the more tempting and goddamn it, now I've got its vivid image burned into my brain. Gross.

Within fifteen minutes of getting to work, I bump into him and he asks me if I want to get a coffee. I don't drink coffee, but I say yes. If he asked me to go for a cup of rat piss, I'd say yes.

He asks me about my weekend and I improvise to seem less dull. Did I go to the Renoir exhibit on Saturday morning? No, but I saw it advertised as I sat on my couch in my pajamas trying to dig out an ingrown hair from my bikini line with tweezers.

The subtle scent of his aftershave makes it very hard to converse. Couldn't I just lick him instead?

Tuesday

I look through the thin bird-shit-tainted window at the stagnant cold, sitting hard against the cement. A thick slab of ham in an Egg McMuffin the size of a car looks back at me from its place on the side of a delivery truck. I can hear the pigeons cooing in confusion as they search for the nest that is no longer since I pitched the wicker chair that housed it. The two eggs Mama pigeon had lain now sit on the terra cotta tiles where I deliberately and gently placed them, so that karma could never accuse me directly of murder.

8:22 a.m. and I cut up a grapefruit and eat it over the sink. Its juice drips down my chin and it's the most luscious part of my day.

I ponder compiling a salad for lunch, but the head of two-week-old romaine and some droopy celery depress me. I want to deserve more.

My bangs will not be tamed and I admire their spirit as much as I curse them and put on a headband, which I then have to change my top to coordinate with.
I brush and floss my grapefruit teeth and wonder how much longer I can put off Botox.

Putting on my boots, gloves, coat and scarf takes enough time to make me late and I rush out the door to seek the migrating bus stop. This city's constant construction has it roaming a two-block radius causing me frustration at an hour too early to be deviating from routine.
Aboard, I am sandwiched between a broad-shouldered suit and a man who might have Downs Syndrome or might just be round-faced and Asian. I turn up the volume on my headphones because Thom Yorke gets me. My stop comes and the others push their way

forward, but I am in no rush until the doors close on me and I swear loudly over the music.

Jolted into reality, I pull the magic music from ears and greet the receptionists. I say good morning to my co-workers, but not too loudly as it is 9:19 according to the T.V. in the elevator and there is no need to draw attention to my tardiness.

Check my e-mail, delete an executive blog from a Toronto big-wig, change into my uncomfortable heels and head to the restroom to look in the mirror and hopefully deem my appearance appealing to his melty brown eyes.

Sometimes I try not to walk by the hallway that I can peek down to see if his coat is hanging at his cubicle. It's my version of hard-to-get. But he was away yesterday and before that was the weekend, so it's been three and a half days without him and I'm desperate for a glimpse of something that assures me I didn't imagine him. His coat will do. It's not there. My heart sinks, but I keep walking, trying to think of an alternate purpose to this trot through the office in my pinching shoes.

I stop to flirt with Dave. He is a reliable source for being objectified when my ego needs a boost.

I say hello to a few other people including Lydia who seems like a friend, but less so when other admin girls are within earshot. Today she just nods since Becky is sitting at the adjacent desk.

I stock the shelves with paper and unload the dishwasher. I crush boxes and take them to recycling.

Lunch time comes and I stand in line at the salad bar where I choose crispy romaine and perky celery. It costs me thirteen bucks.

Every table is full, so I sit beside a man who slurps his noodles and I glare passive aggressively because that is the Canadian way.

I head back to my desk where I bump into my beloved in the hallway before I've had a chance to check my teeth for lettuce. He gives me that twinkly-eyed smile and my day improves drastically. In that moment I don't care about selling out on my dreams to join corporate drudgery. I don't care that that I have a new age spot cleverly disguised as a freckle or that my bills exceed my income by four hundred dollars every month. There is only him. Only the knowledge that under the dress shirt lies a taut bicep with an arty/meaningful tattoo. Only the feeling that getting out of bed this morning suddenly stops seeming futile. Only the hope that maybe tomorrow I will run into him before lunch and that we will share a romantic food court experience where he professes that he has changed his policy about dating co-workers and that we should definitely be together. And then he's passed me and I float back to my desk where a big box of mail sits on my chair.

Wednesday

Today I wake up at 3:00 a.m. and am still awake when my alarm goes off. I do that sometimes, wake up at 3:00 a.m. but usually I'm asleep again just before my alarm goes off. Not today. I contemplate calling in sick. Calling in tired should be an option. I'm useless without sleep, but coming up with a lie seems like more of an effort than just getting dressed. I put together an outfit able to be coordinated with flat shoes because fuck heels when you haven't slept.

Seven Days of Weak

The bus smells like farts and I think about how superior I am for not passing gas on the bus, which is a really ridiculous thing to feel superior about.

When I get to work, the idiot receptionist who met her idiot husband in Narcotics Anonymous asks me for a donation to Jeans Day. She excitedly tells me that I can give a minimum donation of twenty dollars and in exchange I can wear jeans to work next Thursday.

I am annoyed because her enthusiasm is akin to school spirit, and I don't need to be reminded that I still haven't escaped that at 31. Also, I hate being asked for money.

The homeless people are out of control in this rainy city. This one guy I see every day at the corner of Georgia and Howe hunches low and makes a voice that sounds like he's crying, only I know he isn't because like I said, I see him every day and no one cries that much, not even me. The first time I heard that voice I stopped and gave him two bucks and a hug, which is a great way to catch hepatitis or something, but I just felt so sorry for him I might've died if I didn't. The next day he was there again, same routine. He didn't seem to recall that just the day before I'd given him two whole dollars and a warm embrace. I studied him more carefully in the weeks to come and noticed he had a wool coat and sturdy running shoes. Then one day I saw him holding out his hand with a five-dollar bill and several Toonies and Loonies and that was it. He asked for change in his pleading voice and I said, "Are you kidding? You've got more than I do, and I work!"

"I've been here since five am, bitch!"

There will be no more hugs for him.

I walk by the partition that separates us and I can smell my love's Cologne. He told me we can't sleep together as long as we work together. I feel my throat close when I think about it.

I go to the break room and sort the recycling.

At 2:30, he sneaks up behind me and hits the back of my chair. I pretend to be angry and punch his leg as though we're in grade three. It's a silent routine we have down in which he says, 'I like your attention, but I can't admit it' and I say, 'I pretend I'm put out by your need for my attention, but really I love it.'

I told him once that he looked good in blue and he's wearing a blue shirt today, which I'm sure is intentional.

I talk to my boss about getting some pictures framed of buildings the company has sold to hang in the boardroom. It's not the most uninteresting project. My boss is a very cool lady. As someone who has had issue with authority since kindergarten, I can state that as fact.

Thursday

I wake up to the sound of my eardrums creaking like the floorboards of a heritage home, an indication that I have been unsuccessful in fighting off the cold that everyone at the office has been whining about. Because I think I am separate from everyone else, I assumed I was impervious to its evils, but no, the virus is in me writhing around and cackling. I curse the research assistant that lurked within the confines of my cubicle yesterday with his snotty nose and flush cheeks and get up to take some Echinacea. I get back in bed and lay there alternating between anger and pity for myself because there is no one to take care of me.

Beep, beep, beep. The alarm goes off needlessly. My head pounds and I fumble for a Kleenex. I decide that denial will be the best action plan for this cold and I couple my softest cardigan with my sexy secretary skirt and some reasonable heels. Looking like shit when you feel like shit is not a good combination.

By three o'clock I am near tears at my desk. Everything is magnified. The fact that when I saw him in the copy room and he didn't stop his conversation to...I dunno, gently caress my hair, is tragic. He hasn't been here since and I hate that I am so pre-occupied with that.

Friday

7:00 a.m. and I have a tough decision to make. I am sick as hell, but it's Friday and if I stay home today it will be three entire days without him. Can I go that long? If my achy bones and my throbbing sinuses don't kill me, that might. People are in such good moods on Fridays. It's the day of long boozy lunches that turn into after work cocktails and my best chance of his affections.

I haul myself into a sitting position and look in the sliding mirrors on my closet for a minute before collapsing back against my pillow wondering if he's worth it.

By three the brokers are starting to leave for drinks and my head pounds.

He comes by my desk and hits the back of my chair lurching my neck forward and making me nearly throw up in agony.

"You comin' for drinks?"

I turn around and smile when I see he's taken his tie off and undone a button. Praise Jesus, I can see some of his chest hair.

"Sure, I can probably get out of here by 4:30."

"I've got a couple of things to finish up, I'll check in before I go."

"Cool."

I get up in search of Ibuprofen. I pop into my boss's office to see if she has any, but her purse is gone and her computer monitor is on sleep, meaning she's left for the weekend.

I pop down to the make-up counter in the mall, sprucing myself up with sample powders and perfume on my wrists.

I am back at my desk within 20 minutes with no one the wiser. My headache has numbed a little. I feel like two to seven margaritas would definitely take the edge off.

I try to wait for him to come by. I organize my paper clips and throw out a few pens that don't work before I give in and go by his desk. He's not there *and* his coat is gone. Tragedy has ensued.

Dave walks by.

"You gonna let me buy you a drink later?"

"If you're lucky." I keep walking, my anxiety rising.

Did he come by my desk while I was in the mall? Dammit. I should've told him I'd be right back. Then he might've noticed I smelled like perfume though and known it was for him.

I circle the office. Most are gone, but not Lydia.

"Hey, you look nice. How are you?" she practically sings. People are their best selves on Friday afternoons.

"I'm fine. You? You wanna go get a drink?"

"Why are you talking so fast?"

Seven Days of Weak

"Am I?"

She nods. "I can't, my mom is meeting me. We're going to pick out shoes for my sister's wedding and then I think she's making dinner, but a bunch of the guys went to Joeys.

Why don't you go meet up with them?"

"Did you see who went?"

"You mean did your boyyyyyfriend go?"

I had confided my crush to Lydia. I would probably regret it someday. "Shhhh! Obviously."

She lowered her voice. "He ran out saying he had to meet a client, like 10 minutes ago."

"Oh. Huh. Did he say if he was going to Joeys after?"

"Nope. Sorry. I'm a bad detective."

"You've failed me miserably Lydia."

"You should go. It will make Dave happy."

"Nah, I have a headache. Have fun shoe shopping with your mom on a Friday night, nerd."

"Bye!"

We blow each other air kisses.

Rachael Biggs

Saturday

I feel sort of better. I ride my bike around the seawall in the glorious sunshine and feel some hope for being alive.

I get home and make Eggs Benedict and then must lie down on the living room floor because I'm so full, which turns into my vacuuming the living room floor when I notice that it's quite gross in such close proximity to my face.

I meditate, not entirely unsuccessfully. There are moments as I sit in the sunbeam streaming through my window that my ego disappears, but then, of course, he panics with the insecurity that I might not need him anymore and barges in on my peace.

I drive my uninsured car to go see my therapist where I am supremely annoyed to hear for the umpteenth time that I need to let go of my crush if I want to heal my addiction to longing. "Your mother is not coming back," he says.

It makes me cry and I want to find the loophole.

At the grocery store, I see a guy I slept with a couple of times. I really don't want him to see me. He's an actor I used to be in class with and I saw him in a commercial recently. The time before that was at a douchey bar about two weeks after he hadn't called me. I was smashed and made fun of his jacket before yelling at him and kicking him in the shin, which he handled maturely and made it that much more embarrassing. He is with a pretty blonde and I am with my bulky raincoat, pondering sensible cereals.

Saturday traffic is bananas and I forgot to buy bananas. By the time I get home it's 5:30. I put away my groceries and am quite hungry. I devour the entire bag of Bits and Bites I intended to take to work for midday nibbles.

I read my book for an hour and take a nap, which I wake up from at 1:00 a.m. and am therefore awake all night. Fortunately, it's Saturday and I have the luxury of sleeping in.

I go to my desk and look at photos on Facebook of people I haven't seen or cared about for ten years.

My stomach rumbles. I have an orange and some toast, better than an entire bag of Bits and Bites.

I turn on the TV and watch the last hour of an unknown (to me) Woody Allen movie, which really makes me wish I lived in New York in the eighties and was surrounded by neurotic intellectual Jews.

I go back to bed and sleep 'til morning. I have dreams about kicking the shit out of faceless people and I wake up panting.

Sunday

Raining. Pouring. Pouring rain. The headache is back with a vengeance. It's like someone cut all the muscles and tendons in my neck and I'm left with is a limp noodle that is supposed to support this dead weight called my head. Maybe I need a new pillow. Always something I need to buy. When I do my budget, rent is at the forefront, but realistically it should be all the other day-to-day bullshit like pillows, and shampoo, and moisturizer, and a new closet door piece so that the door will close, and dirt to re-pot that plant, and lip balm, and a new frying pan since all the Teflon has chipped off the current one and is probably giving me cancer as we speak.

Life is expensive. I spend a lot of time in the miscellaneous store. A Vietnamese couple make up for their limited English with unlimited miscellaneous items that are all about useful. A while back, I bought a grabber gadget aptly called Grab-it! to reach the jeans I can now store on the top shelf of my closet. It is a goal of mine to add a lower bar in the closet for hanging pants and I made the mistake of trying to explain my desire to the proprietor, but all he could suggest were coat hangers much to my chagrin.

I also buy a stiff yellow broom to clean the pigeon crap off of my deck and a hair catcher for my bathroom drain with the hopes it will cut back on my monthly Draino bill. Remarkable really that I have any hair on my head considering how much goes down the damn drain.

I go for a spray tan. I am frighteningly pale. If I could change one thing about my appearance it would be to have olive skin. The kind that is hairless and freckle-less and never gets sunburned.

My gorgeous brother and his sweet, but pretentious girlfriend come over for pasta. She can only try to be pretentious because they have just moved to the city from small town nowhere, and she is not aware enough of fashion or culture or wealth to actually *be* pretentious. I don't mind her though. She has changed his name from Jamie to James and calls her parents mother and father. It's kind of amusing because she's nineteen. I do my best to horrify her by cursing a lot and calling her Chris instead of Christine. I'm thrilled that my brother has found love. He really deserves it after the horrors our mother put him through.

He and Pretentious Christine brought an apple pie. That was nice. They do everything together. He gave her our Grandma's diamond ring and they say they are engaged.

I walk them to the bus stop and tear up when I hug my very tall brother goodbye. When did we become adults?

9 p.m. and the two days a week I get to be myself are quickly evaporating. I decide to go for a walk, relishing the crisp night air. As I come around the corner to the coffee shop, I am grateful for the five-dollar bill I have tucked in inside my jacket pocket. I feel like a chai. I open the door and before I can turn around and convince

myself it wasn't him, there he is. The back of his head and the black wool coat I know so well holding the hand of a girl three inches shorter than him with honey curls and laughter in her voice.

    I turn away, as my vision blurs. I'll call in sick tomorrow.

Illustrious Longing

Jaqueline's beauty was evident early on. Although she was tall, she was never gangly as most models complain with fake modesty. She carried herself with poise and dignity and from the age of twelve she was sought after by males. This worried her father a great deal and he took it upon himself to show her personally what sort of things boys would try. This role playing got especially uncomfortable when her father was drinking. It made her mother uncomfortable too and she would go in her room and close the door without even cleaning up the dishes from dinner.

When she was fourteen, Jaqueline found a photographer on-line and gave him a hand job in exchange for a photo shoot and she took those pictures and sent them to every modeling agency she found on-line. She got a lot of interest and chose the agent who offered to put her up in an apartment with four other girls her age in New York city.

She sent her grandmother a Christmas card every year, but she deliberately lost contact with her parents.

Jaqueline was ready for a transition. By the time she met Finn, she had dated too many men and each one only reminded her of someone else who had disappointed her.

Finn was a 26-year-old bartender who was born and raised across the bridge and had never moved beyond a ten-mile radius of his parents. He was handsome in an understated way and Jaqueline liked that one of his front teeth was slightly bigger than the other. He lived with two of his three brothers and the other one was married with a baby on the way.

Jaqueline sat down at Finn's bar after a grueling editorial shoot one evening, wearing heavy make-up and with her hair wildly over styled. It was obvious that she was in the business of being sexy and Finn did his best to seem nonchalant about it, as is necessary if you want to have a respectable conversation with someone that is sexy for a living.

Finn poured her a scotch and soda and they talked about the impending election. Jaqueline was impressed with his political prowess and that he blushed when she touched his arm. She wrote her number on the napkin before she left and exited smiling.

Their romance burned bright and hot and ignited a desire that Jaqueline had never felt.

Her gentlemen suitors to date had been anything but gentlemanly. They were usually businessmen of considerable means, so as to level the playing field with her beauty or hotshot artists who slept with models as validation or because it was hip. Finn had a lovely innocence by comparison, and he stayed in her hotel room for thirty-nine consecutive nights. They would sleep all day and when he came home from work at 3 a.m. they would walk around the city laughing and kissing and never letting go of one another's hand. She took only one job that month and because it was in Milan and sounded very romantic, she bought him a ticket and insisted he feign strep throat in order to join her. One enchanted evening after they had shared gelato, Finn took her face in his hands and told her he loved her. Jaqueline cried and he made her laugh by taking off his shirt, right there on the cobbled street and offering it to her to wipe her nose.

Jaqueline no longer felt exhausted. Everything seemed possible now. She indulged her daydreams by looking at homes to buy on-line—a sprawl in North Carolina with Willow trees ideal for a swing, a quaint Victorian in San Francisco with more varieties of flowers in the garden than she had ever seen, and a classic Cape Cod with a row boat out front.

When they got back from Italy, Finn wanted to spend the night at his own place.

"Why?" Jaqueline protested vehemently.

"I haven't hung out with my brothers in nearly a month; I miss them."

"But, I'll be so lonely." She put on her best pouty face, which was really a top-of-the-line pouty face because she had rehearsed it so many times for photo shoots. "It's just one night, babe. I've been with you non-stop since we met. Be cool, Sugarbear." He took her in his arms and tried to console her.

"Oh, am I not cool enough for you now? You think you can do better?" She pushed him away and locked herself in the bathroom while hating herself for being so embarrassingly weak.

Finn was puzzled as he tried to reason with her through the bathroom door, but she was silent and eventually he grew frustrated with her immaturity and let himself out.

When Jaqueline got it together about three hours later, she called Finn, but it went straight to voicemail. She realized she'd overreacted and decided to try again in case he hadn't heard the ring.

Over and over she dialed and when Finn saw her number for the fourth time, he switched his phone to silent. He needed a minute to breathe. He had never experienced a woman like this. He valued simplicity. He'd had three serious long-term relationships in his twenty-six years and all of them had remained friends.

Jaqueline was a different animal. There was nothing simple about her and the complexities that were initially titillating and her seeming sophistication seemed more and more out of his league with each missed call.

By morning Jaqueline was nearly hysterical. Her body convulsed as though it were being shocked with electricity. She had experienced rage, humiliation, sadness, fear, desperation and yearning and was finally left with a gut churning loneliness that had always been there, but had been safely stowed away for a very long time. It made her teeth itch. It made her skin feel too tight. It made the most ordinary things in the following days an impossibility.

She got in touch with a drug dealer who helped her spiral further into her depression.

She gave up calling Finn in an effort to preserve self-respect but the agony was unbearable and she *had* to see him. She rented a car and waited for him to get off work, then followed him home. She did this every night for two weeks and on the nights he was off she would sit outside his apartment in her different rental cars hoping to catch a glimpse, or sometimes just waiting for a light to come on or go off.

One night Finn came out of his house with a mousy blonde. She was short, barely reaching his bicep, and she wore a gaudy jacket. At first Jaqueline convinced herself this must be a relative or maybe a friend, but certainly not her replacement, until he walked the mousy bitch to her car and kissed her on the lips. Tears welled up in Jaqueline's eyes but she would not be her mother, she would not! She wiped the tears away and a jealous rage took over. The mouse pulled out, and Finn stood at the curb waving as Jaqueline revved her engine and screeched into traffic.

Finn saw Jaqueline but shook his head and assured himself that it couldn't be her. She didn't even drive. She'd had drivers her entire adult life and what would she be doing over here? She never left Manhattan.

The mouse was blissfully content as she drove. She turned her music up and sang along. She and Finn had remained friends since they dated in high school, the same high school where she now taught and fondly remembered him every time she walked by their adjacent lockers. He had called her last week telling her that he wanted to see her and she had readily agreed. They fit. They always had. She practiced writing her first name with his last, just as she had done back when they dated for those three years when they were 16. She giggled to herself as she thought about it now.

Jaqueline's heart was racing. She opened the sunroof to try and breathe more freely, but she could not. She felt dizzy, but her focus remained on the car in front of her, so much so that she didn't notice it was about to stop at the light and she thrust into the back of it at a startling speed. Smashing her face into the steering wheel shook her from her craziness for a moment and she realized that if she had to get out and exchange information with this nothing of a woman that it would get back to Finn and that was unthinkable. Before the mouse could get out of her car, Jaqueline reversed and did a U-turn heading back to the city. There were no cars around.

Being that it was rental, Jaqueline had to pay a considerable sum of money to have the car fixed before she took it back, but Jaqueline made considerable sums of money, so that was not an issue.

When Finn didn't hear from his sweetheart, he grew worried. They had a pact since 10th grade that she would call as soon as she got home, washed her face, brushed her teeth and got into bed. First call of the day, last one at night was their nauseating little rule. He had relearned exactly the time this took over the past week and he knew that nearly two hours was much too long. He called her all night and in the morning he went to her apartment and rang the buzzer. When there was no answer, he called her mom, who was sobbing and had to pass the phone to her dad. The unthinkable. Mouse was in a hit and run accident. Her neck was broken and she died instantly.

Finn flashed back to the white Porshe Cayenne that screeched down his street. Jaqueline. He went back in his call log and dialed her number. He tried the hotel's front desk, but she had checked out. She was nowhere to be found and he felt a desperation similar to hers when he would not take her calls just six weeks ago.

Rainbows and Lollipops

The garden is overgrown. Low maintenance cacti prevail and a tangle of dried-up vines threaten to swallow the purple door. I rip off the note he's scrawled: *Come on in, the water's warm!* and with it a large swatch of paint, which I toss in the sandy dirt.

I flip off my flip flops and walk down the hall.

I can hear the shower running and him singing.

"Cuz I try and I try and I try and I try and I try and I tryyyy."

He's trying too hard, as usual. Mick Jagger only tried four times before succumbing to the fact that he couldn't get no satisfaction.

He is in the shower at precisely the time I am scheduled to arrive to let me know that his chubby little cock is clean and ready to suck.

There are naked photos of a trashy blonde with balloon-like implants on his computer screen. I pretend not to see them because I know he wants me to.

I hear the shower door close and he lumbers in with nothing but a hopeful look in his eyes.

"Hey, you! Lookin' good as usual!"

If this were what I usually looked like, it would be cause for concern. My hair is oily, and I have been wearing my T-shirt dress since this morning when I used the dirt I'd pilfered from the community garden to plant the petunias that I'd been collecting from the walkways late at night. No one would miss the flowers since they grew like weeds and the rich folks had their gardeners replace them every 6 weeks anyways.

I look good compared to him though, if we are basing his compliment in relativity.

Rainbows and Lollipops

Wide pink stretch marks crisscross his gut, loose moles hang around his neck, his nostrils are flared like a bull waiting to charge and doughy kneecaps nearly buckle under his weight, making him a sight few would call 'good as usual'.

He wants a hug. I can feel it shooting from behind the pathetic longing that are his eyeballs. A hug is not what I have in mind though.

I'm thinking more of ramming the heel of my hand upwards into his nose and then laughing joyfully as he falls backward into the fireplace and I stomp on the four pounds of testicles that swing between his mushy thighs.

I set up my massage table, accidentally glancing at the twit on the computer screen, as he looks on expectantly.

"You like her?" he asks.

"I don't know her."

"She's a friend of a friend. My friend spends time with her and thought I might like her. I think she's a prostitute."

"That's fairly evident, yes."

He's doing two things: he's letting me know that he has other options thereby trying to get a reaction of competitiveness while also aiming to incite a conversation about prostitution.

He's hoping that maybe that will turn into some liberal leaning heart-to-heart in which I decide that's it's cool to fuck him for money.

I choke down my vomit to speak. "Prostitutes are the safest people you can sleep with next to porn actresses."

"Why's that?"

"Because they're professionals. They always use condoms."

"Do you like sex with condoms?"

I'd like to pull a giant condom over his head and get my satisfaction watching him flail and choke to death because his fingers are too fat to find its edge to free himself.

"Okay, hop on the table." I say with caustic pep.

There is no such thing as hopping for him though; there is only hoist and roll.

I stare at the metal filing cabinets as my reluctant hands move down his ample back. Stray hairs, a puss-filled whitehead and a scaly texture greet my fingers and palms as I apologize silently to them.

I will deposit the two hundred and fifty dollars to my account immediately upon leaving here and finally being able to pay the minimum on my credit card before being charged a thirty-five-dollar late fee again. I can also get the oil changed in my car if that mailer I got hasn't expired. Will that make the light go out?

I get down to his ass and he moans and clears his throat. "I make sure I wash real good every time before you come over in case you want to go deeper."

Is there a bat anywhere in this room? Anything sharp? Oooh, that metal ruler. That would work. It's an odd shape, but maybe if I put some of this oil on it first and use force...

"Why would I want to do that?"

"Oh, in case you want to get deeper into the muscles."

"There are no muscles in your butt crack."

"You sure? Best to double check."

A bat would be better. A bat with spikes. I'll make one. I'll plan ahead next time. Fail to plan, plan to fail.

He laughs nervously, knowing not to push me again for now. He's conveniently forgotten that he's encouraged me before to get closer to the most unfathomably grotesque part of his physique and that I've given him a firm no.

It is time for the dreaded flip-over. His prick has emerged slightly from its rolls of blubber and drips with a translucent slime that nearly makes me gag. I wipe it roughly before getting a grip and focusing again on the filing cabinet.

I could puke all over him and this table and this room right now. I could drown him in thick, steamy vomit and get double satisfaction as he slides into its pool on the floor writhing like a puffer fish yanked from an aquarium.

"Tell me what you're thinking about," he coos.

"Rainbows and lollipops."

"You're hilarious!"

Rainbows and Lollipops

It takes him a minute to get hard. If I'd done his arms by pulling them up over his head and letting him fondle me with his sausage fingers, he would have been fully erect, but I don't need him commenting on my tampon.

I roll his four inches of flesh in my hands like I'm making gnocchi and then grab it like my gear shift, as he exhales deeply and I bury my nose in my armpit in an effort to dodge the rancid odor.

"Grab tighter," he whispers. "Tight like your pussssy."

Would my hands be able to grab tight enough around his neck to cut off his air or would the fat get in the way? How hard would I have to squeeze? As hard as he is squeezing my ass right now?

I clench my cheeks together, so he can't slip his hand in anywhere and think about which ATM I will go to when my freedom is restored. The parking on Sepulveda is free, but will my car make it that far without oil?

"You have the best ass in America," he hisses.

He jerks and convulses on the table and I think maybe we're getting to the end, but he's just being dramatic. Fucking L.A. with all of its unrealized actors.

"Slow down," he says. "As if your mouth is just pulling me up, pulling me up, pulling me up, up, up."

If I can't successfully choke him would he be able to get up quickly enough to defend himself? I could definitely run faster than him. Would he chase me out into the road? Nah.

I slow my tug obediently, desperately wanting this to end as much as my aching forearm does.

"Squeeze my balls. Real tight, like."

I grip a handful of the hairy flab as it oozes between my fingers in rebellion, shifting my weight, stepping on something sharp. I look down at potato chip crumbs without an ounce of surprise.

"Tighter!" he grunts.

Next time he leans in for a hug/grope I will stick him with a knife I have concealed in my sleeve. Maybe in the neck. I will research where the jugular is, so my efforts aren't wasted on a surface wound, and I will quickly step out of the way so as not to get blood on myself when it starts to spurt like a faucet needing its washer replaced. Then I will stand over him as he thrashes about, much like he is now, only dying and confused, and I will say all the things I've been wanting to say. Don't ever ask me for a hug again motherfucker! Stop fucking pushing me. Take a hint! I don't want to touch your asshole! I would rather pour acid in my eyes than see you naked. Put some fucking clothes on! You make me sick! Do you see me? Do you see that even with my greasy hair and my gardening clothes that I would never ever, EVER be attracted to you? Are you fucking stupid? Are you a fucking moron? Yes, you are! You are a stupid, shallow, moron that likes me only for my body, but I hate you for so much more than yours. I hate you because I'm here. I hate that partying became more important to me than high school and that I never had the urge to 'apply myself' as my teachers suggested. I hate that I deserve so much better, but that eventually I won't if I keep coming here. Slowly this will become normal and as you continue to push or offer me more money, I might succumb. I will stab myself in the jugular if that ever happens.

He continues to thrash about on the table, getting my hopes up.

Do it! Do it now! Come, you fat fucking fuck!

Finally, one hundred thousand years later, he squirms on the table and his legs raise up stiffly as thick yellow snot exits his vile organ. He whinnies like a horse and before he can open his eyes, I am in the bathroom washing my hands with enough soap to drown in.

I don't look in the mirror.

Burning

My three uncles walk me down the grassy aisle; Derek on my left arm tears up, Roddy squeezes my right elbow, trying to make me laugh, and Brian is two steps behind because he promised my dad he'd always have my back.

Your mum's beloved garden surrounds us, filling the air with the sweetness we emulate on this cloudless day.

Your niece and nephew, dressed in their colorful finest, grin widely, showcasing braces and missing teeth that are deeply endearing. I'm so excited to share your family with you and so grateful that you come with them, though you alone are so much more than enough.

The dress your sister sewed for me swishes silky soft against my bare legs like a posse of garden nymphs are gently exhaling on its skirt. I am stylish and sexy in a demure way that I can see in your liquid brown eyes drives you wild with desire. Your periwinkle linen suit creases at the hip bone where you've crossed your legs at some point before getting to the gazebo your brothers built for this occasion. Under its fresh pine smell is where we begin our wedded life and if there is such thing as perfection, today is it.

There will be no drunk plus ones, or distant relatives. We have gleefully skipped past stuffy hotel bars and indifferent caterers. Everything is familiar in the best possible way; the way it was when we met. We talked for three hours that night and nearly ten the next. I'll never tire of talking to you, but first let's say the two most important words: I do, I do, I dooooo!

"It's burning?" Hannah's lilting Ukrainian accent cuts in.

"Oh, uh, no, I'm okay."

"Your eyes are watering."

"Sorry. I was just thinking of something happy. I mean sad."

"Happy-sad."

"Right."

"You're like me; I cry at everything now. It's my age."

I'm sure she's no older than 30, but okay. I push out a gasping sound meant to be a laugh trying not to open my eyes and go blind from the lash tint solution she's applying. To go blind of vanity would be like a biblical story of punishment for the sin of being engrossed in outer beauty and I'd really rather not.

You used to make fun of me for how long it took to choose shoes or how many bags I packed to go away for the weekend, as if you would've preferred a rugged girl with minimal toiletries for her unkempt skin and one pair of Blundstone that she wore with everything, but I'm not near as high maintenance as you think. Sure, I like my eyelashes to pop, but I'm not obsessed with appearances. My daydream of our unpretentious and elegantly understated nuptials is proof of that.

Rachael Biggs

    I hope the statute of limitations on your disgust for me is up soon and that my love for you stops churning your stomach bile. Unblock your heart and my DMs. Let's talk like we used to. We have a wedding to plan.

Peg and Pete's Precarious Predicament

When Peg opened the door at 5:43pm every weeknight, she was greeted with a whistle that flattered her without fail. Peter would wait the thirty-six seconds it took her to remove her shoes, hang her hemp satchel on the hook behind the door and plunk down at the kitchen table before he hopped over and called out enthusiastically, "Hello, gorgeous!"

His sincerity always made her blush.

She held out her arm for him to get closer and hear about her day.

"Marley was late again. That's three times this week and it's only Thursday." Pete shook his head in distaste and Peg nodded in agreement.

"She had on a dress that I'm sure I saw at Goodwill last weekend, but of course I didn't say I knew she was lying when I overheard her telling Kim she'd paid $130 for it.

Peter looked aghast as he listened intently.

"For lunch I had the Salisbury steak leftovers. Quite good. They really get better after sitting in the fridge overnight. More tender. I'm going to make the chicken tonight. Should be thawed by now." She went over and opened the refrigerator.

"Supper, supper, supper!" Pete screeched, letting her know to step on it.

Peg laughed and removed a lettuce leaf from the bag where she had carefully separated, washed, and patted them dry before storing them between two damp paper towels in the crisper.

"Start with a salad, shall we?" she said holding out a leaf for him.

Peg and Pete's Precarious Predicament

After they'd eaten and chatted some more, Peg put on her flannel pajamas (flannel for now, cotton for summer) and the twosome settled into the recliner to watch some television. Peg was fond of the history channel. The depictions of ancient societies and their ruins fueled her occasional fantasies about being an archaeologist.

Pete, on the other hand, loved violence. Anything with a car chase, or something blowing up, had the same effect as it does on most domesticated males—sheer titillation. On occasion, the history channel would cover a war gone by and in those instances the couple were in agreement. Pete had an uncanny talent for mimicking sound effects that always made Peg laugh. On the rare occasion that a nature program could be found, there was no argument either, but there seemed to be less and less of them, as if everything about lions and gorillas and giraffes had already been explored. As soon as Peg got up to use the bathroom, Pete would use his beak to turn the sound to near deafening volume. Peg would scold him before regaining control of the remote and Pete would comply because this is what compromise consists of.

The duo's weekends consisted of three to five activities from the following list: working in the garden; the assembly of a puzzle; reading; looking out the window at Mrs. Fleming's cat chasing something innocent, an activity more a habit of Pete's arrogant fondness due to the thin pane of glass separating him and the ferocious beast; vacuuming; ironing; folding laundry; baking and always on Sundays, grocery shopping for the week.

On this particular Sunday Peg filled her cart with all the usual staples and twelve ears of sweet corn because it was on sale and can be frozen.

Making her way to the register, she unloaded her cart methodically, careful to keep like items together for efficiency and because she suspected if she were a cashier, she would appreciate the customer's co-operation with this.

Peg placed her peach yogurt on the conveyor belt with a little regret that her favorite flavor—raspberry, had so many seeds. Seeds were more Pete's forte she chuckled to herself, imagining him relishing a container of raspberry yogurt while she looked on in envy.

"All these clouds gettin' you down, ma'am?"

Peg looked up from the sticky beige stain on the floor with the hairball stuck in it to a cashier she'd never seen before with a name tag that read "Tony" in small block letters. His red and white uniform still had its creases, as if recently released from its constrictive packaging and sat awkwardly on his slight frame. He had clean-cut hair that you might call strawberry blonde and a face that seemed to smile of its own volition. Folks would smile at him because they thought he was smiling at them and he in turn, would smile, giving him instant likability and as a result, a pretty positive outlook on life.

Peg nodded politely to say hello to Tony, but since she had the type of face that hardly showed a mile-wide grin, the kindly cashier took it upon himself to inquire about the state of her mood.

"I'm sorry, pardon me?" she said confused by his question.

"I've been here nearly two weeks and I haven't seen a lick a sunshine."

"Oh, the weather. Yes."

He was bagging her twelve cobs of corn. "Having dinner guests tonight, are we?"

Peg let out a little sound that couldn't quite be distinguished.

"Oh, no. They were just... just on sale. Twelve for three dollars." Her thriftiness embarrassed her slightly.

"I'll let you in on a little secret," he said leaning in, allowing Peg to smell the crisp scent that made her feel like she suddenly knew him quite a bit better. "You can get as few as you like." He paused, as if to build suspense. "They're still only 25 cents each. Just between you and me though." He winked and Peg felt a joyful rush of tingles shoot through her body.

She looked at the twelve bulky husks of corn and thought about the work of shucking them and the mess it would make. The thought that followed was so quick, you might say it was all one thought. It was of Pete squawking merrily as he dissected a cob, kernel by kernel.

"My friend Pete, he loves corn on the cob."

"Aha, Pete is the guest of honor tonight, is he?"

"Oh, no, we live together."

"Oh, I see."

His demeanor shifted ever so slightly, and Peg knew that he didn't see at all. "Pete is a parrot."

"Oh, he's your pet. Neato! My uncle had a bird for a few years."

Pete was *much* more than a pet, but something about Tony's eyes kept her from being as offended as she might have been. Instead, she launched into a lengthy explanation of Pete's unique coloring, his extensive vocabulary and about how, when she'd got him at thirteen, from her eccentric aunt on her father's side, he was barely the size of her hand and nearly all gray and how, with each new brightly colored feather, he seemed to understand Peg better than the day before.

Tony listened intently as she talked. He knew that everyone liked to talk about themselves, especially those who appeared shy at first. He enjoyed being the one to bring them out of them out of their shell, simply by listening. His grandma loved to remind him as a child that he had two ears and one mouth and the adage had won him friends time and again.

Over his years in working with the public, he'd noticed that the Chatty Cathys of the world talked about a whole lot of nothing. He feigned polite interest in their kid's grades, their upcoming birthday parties and who they were entertaining for the holidays, but those who talked the most were really the ones who needed to put a sock in it. Someone like Peg, well, she was a different breed. Her initial timid manner, juxtaposed with the lively dissertation on her bird, were... intriguing, and so at the at the end of it, Tony suggested that perhaps she'd like to introduce the two of them and she impulsively agreed, later questioning her sanity for it when nerves overcame her.

Two days later on the day they'd arranged to meet, Peg attempted to apply mascara. She'd managed to poke both of her eyes with the wand rendering them quite red and worrying Pete that she'd been crying. When her cheerful morning mood showed its usual self, however, he decided she must just be tired from shucking all that corn the night before. If parrots were capable of sighing in relief he would have done just that, but instead he gave her a welcome compliment by calling out, "Pretty lady!

Pretty lady!" as she put on her coat and smiled the smile he'd spot a mile away.

When Peg walked down the wet steps of the library at 5:05, Tony was waiting at the bottom just as he'd said he would be. The excitement she'd been feeling all day turned to anxiety and she thought about dashing back into the safety of the bookshelves but then he waved and smiled, or maybe he made no expression at all, but he certainly appeared to be smiling and she knew there was no turning back.

"Hiya!"

"Oh, hi." It seemed to Peg that the voice box of a pubescent boy had been implanted in her throat. She cleared it loudly, and then again.

"How are you?" she asked.

"Oh, I'm real good. Had a good day. Went for a long ride this morning."

"A ride?"

"Yeah, yeah, I took my bike up to Lakewood Trail about eight thirty this morning and was up there 'til nearly noon—great view of the channel. You ever been?"

"Oh, no, not me."

"What do you like to do?"

Peg thought about it for a minute and shrugged. What did she like to do? "Oh, I dunno. This and that."

The pair stopped and Tony bought them each a fancy coffee drink that Peg enjoyed nearly as much as this nice man's company. By the time they got to Peg's little brown house it was 6:27.

Pete was befuddled. Feeling he'd exhausted his options, he was waiting on the coat rack beside the front door. He'd flown around the house numerous times wondering if it were possible he hadn't heard Peg come in. He'd scoured the bedroom, the bathroom and the laundry area in the back. Finally, he'd settled here on the coat rack, still doubting his judgment that his mistress was just plain late.

When the door flung open and Pete chastised Peg loudly it startled Tony, causing him to jump back, subsequently hitting his head on the door jam. It was a bad first impression for them both.

"Oh gosh! I'm so sorry, he's not usually so boisterous!"

Pete was ready to accept the apology until he realized it was not *he* who was being apologized to at all, but rather this white-skinned trespasser. He flew into the living room to sulk.

Tony, ever good-natured, assured Peg that it was no big deal. The ice was officially broken when Peg could no longer suppress a giggle and when Tony joined in, they were sharing their first laugh.

Peg got out the kettle and made them some tea with fresh mint from her green house. She showed him the greenhouse and explained that she'd built it from a kit she'd bought at the hardware store and that it was actually quite simple.

Like any infidelity, Peg was having such a nice time, that Pete and their daily routines had not crossed her mind.

"So, let's meet this bird of yours, shall we? I think I'm starting to get hearing back in my left ear."

Peg's eyes darted to the clock and like an adulterer scrambling for her pants, she leaped up.

"Oh, I can't believe it. I've got to feed Petey. Just give me a minute. I'll be right in."

"Oh, yeah. Does he have a real set dinner-time, like?"

Peg looked at him as though he'd asked something absurd like: "Do you need to breathe air in order to live?" She shook her head as politely as she could muster.

"We always eat at six."

"O.K., well I'll let you hop to it then."

"Oh, but it will just take a minute. Here, uh, take these peanuts. They're his favorite. I'm going to chop up this apple and we can take it in to him together."

At first, when they entered the living room, Pete was not visible.

"Petey....Pete? Where are you?" Peg called out guiltily. She looked around a minute.

"Hmm, that's weird." Then she saw the curtain moving and realized what he'd done. He was sitting on the sill of the window, hidden by the curtains she'd worked so hard on not more than a month ago, while systematically dismantling their threads, one by one.

His revenge tactic infuriated her. Under ordinary circumstances, there would have had to have been an immediate punishment, probably confinement to his cage, however the circumstance of having a man in her house was so extraordinary that Peg gritted her teeth instead.

"Suppertime," she called out.

Pete popped his head out from behind the curtain. He was famished and allowed it to override his pride, as he hopped onto the coffee table and raised an apple chunk to his mouth with his talon.

Tony sat down on the couch, and in an attempt to reconcile with Pete, began cracking the shells of the peanuts for the curmudgeonly bird.

Pete looked at the peanuts and then to Peg. Her anger over the curtains dissolved into compassion.

"He likes to do it himself. It's kind of his favorite part of the whole experience."

Tony dropped the peanut. "Sorry, pal." He spoke in a voice normally reserved for imbeciles or Chihuahuas.

Peg sat down on the couch next to Tony. Tony smiled as he watched Peg gaze lovingly at Pete.

While Tony watched Peg, Pete watched Tony. He looked at Peg the way the men on the animal shows zoomed in on the gorillas. Sometimes those men took photos of the gorillas and made friends with the baby gorillas and other times they shot them with rifles or spears. Which type of man was this? Pete couldn't discern.

Peg seemed to be moving closer to Tony and Tony didn't seem to mind. And then, in an instant, three things occurred. Someone attempted a kiss. Someone else, caught off guard, quickly recoiled from the prospect and someone else lunged at Tony's face with either protective instincts or blind jealousy.

A sharp black beak seared into Tony's eye socket and Peg screamed. Tony flailed his arms in front of him, doing his best to protect himself from further assault, but there was no need. Pete, filled with substantially more regret than the other two, flew around the room in a panic. He ran into the wall, knocked over Peg's mother's wedding vase and defecated, for the first time ever, on the carpet.

Peg and Pete's Precarious Predicament

When Tony's one good eye registered the terror on Peg's face, he matched it.

"Help!! Oh Jesus, help!" he squeaked, leaning forward. A yellow gooey substance seeped between his fingers, before it turned to blood and Peg had to turn her head, for fear she'd vomit. "Ahhhh.... oh, God! Do something! Help!" he shouted now.

She ran to the bathroom to find a towel, then stopped and thought maybe she should call 911 instead, but the blood made her go back for the towel first.

"Oh God, do something. Do something! Help!" Tony yelped.

"I, I—I don't know what to do!" She had started to cry now. Pete went to her and tried to perch on her shoulder, but she wouldn't stand still and instead his wings just flapped into her face making matters worse. She reached out with the towel for Tony, but with the bird hovering around, he shooed her away in fear.

"What should I do? I don't know what to do!" she whimpered.

"Just stay away from me! Both of you!" His panic was mounting as he batted the air with the hand that

107.

wasn't clutching his eye. He turned in a circle twice, trying to get his bearings before he staggered toward the door, emitting a wail as he walked first into the coat rack.

Peg stood in horror and Pete was finally able to land on her shoulder briefly before she lunged for the door vigorously locking both locks.

The two were silent then—trying to fathom the doom that was upon them. Within minutes, ear-piercing sirens extinguished any hopes of denial. Pete imitated them, as he did when he'd heard them on television and Peg relinquished her earlier restraint, unleashing her anger now. "Sshh! Peter. Hush up!"

Sensing that this was not the time to challenge her, he was instantly silenced by her request. Peg, not breathing, spied stealthily behind the shelter of the recently shredded curtain. Her hand went to her mouth and she gasped as she saw Tony, his face dramatically bandaged, being wheeled from Mrs. Fleming's house on a stretcher. She knew she should go out there, explain what had happened and make sure Tony was okay, but she was paralyzed with fear. What would they think of Pete? How would she defend this?

Pete landed on the windowsill and not wanting him to be spotted, Peg lifted him to her shoulder. He was overcome with relief from the physical closeness and nuzzled his head into her hair, afraid to see what was happening beyond their four walls.

Peg closed the tattered curtains as the ambulance pulled away, and proceeded to pace with Pete on her shoulder, all the while yearning desperately for her formal uneventful existence.

"Think. We've got to think, what to do," she muttered to her friend.

Pete repeated, "Think, think, think," as if this might help.

Before long there was an assertive knock at the door.

"Who is it?"

"Animal services ma'am."

She and Pete exchanged a contrite look.

"We have reason to believe there's a dangerous animal on the premises."

Peg slapped her hand over her mouth. "Uh, just a minute." She raised her finger to her lips to keep Pete from incriminating them both.

She took Pete from her shoulder and cradled him in the cups of her hands, the way she had when he was just a baby. She felt the familiar weight of his warm breast beneath his glorious bright feathers. He lay still, as if surrendering to his fate, but his eyes pleaded, for what he didn't know.

Peg went to the window of her bedroom and pried it open with one hand while Pete repositioned himself.

The knock on the door persisted and Peg kissed her beloved on the head and he lifted his talon for a stoic good-bye in the form of a handshake. He turned then and flew through the open window into the fading glow of the orange sky as Peg went to answer the door.

Cyanide Soup

As I sat in the stairwell to put on my running shoes, she continued to natter.

"You shouldn't have done that. You *really* shouldn't have done that. You've upset the kids. Jamie was so upset he had tears in his eyes. You shouldn't have done that."

I pulled up my socks, the craggy hag hovering over me, her voice getting shriller with each non-sensical thing she said.

"I would have told them when it was time. It wasn't the right time. You upset them for no reason. You *shouldn't* have done that."

Her bony ankles stuck out between the mint green pants that were too short for her and the thread-bare half socks, that barely covered the bottom of her feet and therefor had no purpose whatsoever.

How easily I could have knocked her down and made this horror stop, but there are laws about killing your 89-year-old grandmother, no matter how enraged she makes you with 40 years of manipulation and bold-faced lies.

"They're just kids! You shouldn't have done that."

"They're not kids, they have kids of their own. Letting them know what's happening is *normal*." I spoke slowly, laying the condescension on thick.

"It is NOT! Don't tell your kids my business!"

I gritted my teeth, wanting to be right in spite of her delirium.

"I don't have kids, Grandma."

"I know!"

She always knew. You could deliver groundbreaking news, top secret CIA intel and she'd say, 'I know'.

Cyanide Soup

She leered at me, face contorted with an ugly anger, her mouth a wrinkled hole of hell surrounded by coral-colored lipstick.

"You shouldn't have DONE that!"

I stood up and she turned her back, still muttering as she stepped up into the laundry room. I picked up my black Nike's with the stitching prematurely unraveling on the left toe and lunged for her but caught myself just as she turned and bore her cold blue eyes into me.

"You were going to hit me!," she shrieked.

Was I? Oh, God. I had to get the fuck out of here.

I stepped around her in the doorway as she shuffled and shifted unpredictably like an annoying Poodle underfoot.

"I'm going to go for a walk."

"Get out and *stay* out!" she said hoarsely.

I slammed the flimsy wooden door behind me, not meaning to, but I was a brute in this 150-year-old house seemingly built for elves. I stepped into the clean Spring air, invigorated by its cool and the scent of lilacs from the tree under which my dead mother lay.

The quiet swooshed over me and I was wrapped in relief. I could hear my breath as I walked quickly away from the dementia demon that inhabited my mother's mother.

I didn't want to go to Ben's. I didn't want him to know how disgusting my family was. I might tarnish the sweetness budding between us for a second time. When we had courted last, I leaned hard on him and regretted it when he told me he couldn't give me what I needed, and so I vowed to need less this time.

Had I not rushed out without my phone I would have called my dad. He would have answered on the first the ring "Hello, Princess," maybe with his most amusing Cockney accent, telling me not to cry. Having been in-laws briefly, he would have understood how the word insane did not begin to describe these people and he would have picked me up in his smokey truck and I would have sat close to him with his arm around me, while he made it all better just by existing. Had I not rushed out without my phone and had I not witnessed his last rattling breath as black goopy blood poured out of his nose and mouth and his hand gripped mine, everything would be more or less okay, but I did, and it wasn't.

I walked down the hill toward the beach. It was a calm June evening with skies as blue as her vacant eyes. The chill of Spring lingered, but Summer was within reach and I marveled at the radiance of the sparkles on the ocean; such a sharp contrast to the dark little house at the top of the hill.

I sat on a brown plastic bench, bubbling with rage. Having come to the island for a film job and to be closer to Ben with the bonus of advancing my career, four months of belongings were inside my grandparent's house and while I couldn't bear the thought of going back there, I had to be on set the next morning and needed my things.

I walked up and down the beach trying to navigate balance in the rocky terrain. She might not let me back in. Maybe she'd barricade the door with a dresser like my mom had when my boyfriend and I went to a movie and she got drunk out of her mind. The lilac didn't fall far from the tree.

As dusk took over and the shining sun carried on to faraway lands, I had to make a move, and as much as I disliked it, that move was going to have to be to go back and get my stuff.

While I walked, I took breaths so deep my lungs wondered if they'd been kidnapped by a blue whale.

The streetlights came on as I approached, and I looked carefully at the home that I'd been coming to for over 30 years. Originally, it had been my great grandmother's house—a two-bedroom rancher on a nice chunk of land with an ocean view. White English roses poked through thorns alongside poppies and daffodils and tulips in every variety and color in spite of the deer that munched on them every chance they got. A clematis grew up and over the cedar roof, its fist-sized purple flowers creeping further and further out of bounds. There was wood paneling throughout, and delicate ceramic things, hand embroidered pillow cases and tiny teacups. When Grandpa's mom started to get too old to look after herself, he and my grandma built a modern addition on top of her tiny home and had lived there ever since. The addition seemed to make the ceilings lower downstairs

Cyanide Soup

and though my 4"10 great-grandmother probably didn't notice, I felt like a giant at 5"7.

The door, surprisingly, was open and I turned the wiggly copper handle and went in. I crept to the back bedroom and started to gather my things as quietly as I could, hoping maybe she hadn't heard me enter. Before I was halfway packed, she was at the bedroom door, hovering and chastising.

"You can't pull those drawers out so far out, they'll fall."

"Okay," I said, keeping my head down, doing my best not to engage.

"I want you out."

"I know, Grandma."

I continued to gather my clothes and put them into the sturdy plastic bins I'd traveled with. She continued to loiter like a vulture, waiting for me to do something she could verbally disapprove of.

"I want the key back."

Ugh, I forgot I had tucked it into the pocket of my hoodie before I left with the violence of an hour ago coursing through my veins. I rummaged through my suitcase and pulled out the key, tossing it on the floor without speaking, still on my knees.

"Don't throw it at me!"

I repeated in my mind: stay calm, be cool, stay calm, be cool.

"I know you're worried and you haven't slept much, but are you sure this is what you want?" I asked through gritted teeth. "

I slept just *fine*!"

"Grandpa's not coming home from the hospital this time. It's normal that you're not feeling quite right."

"I feel just fine."

I struggled to close the zipper of my suitcase, unsure how clothes always seemed to expand when packing, but shrink when trying to do up zippers on tight jeans.

"You won't see me again," I said flatly, aiming to sting.

She crossed her arms, her eyes steely as tears streamed down my face and I turned my head away from her.

I got everything out of the bedroom and went to the kitchen where I packed my vitamins and wrapped my favorite mug in the sleeve of a sweater she'd knit for me.

She climbed the stairs on all fours to accommodate her arthritis, finally leaving me in peace while I packed my shoes, wondering why the hell I brought so many pairs. I slunk out, my arms weighted with bags and my hands full. I didn't look at the house as I drove away, knowing she'd be in the upstairs window.

Ben's studio was 40 seconds away and the only sensible thing to do was to go there and give him an abridged version of what happened. I would get a hotel, but I needed a hug first and to talk to someone with all their marbles.

He was sitting on the couch quietly re-stringing a guitar, his face full of peaceful concentration.

"Hi," I said smiling like nothing was out of the ordinary.

His face lit up, thank fuck. "I wasn't expecting you—hey!"

His boyishness made me feel light. It was #46 in the compilation of times I knew I loved him.

He made me a bagel and I sat close. It was hard to swallow, but I knew I'd be hungry if I didn't.

Buzzing with adrenaline and exhaustion by the time I found my way to the hotel, I negotiated a monthly rate that was more than half my salary. I ran a bath and lay in the bubbles, trying to comprehend the years of resentment that had come to a head only a couple of hours earlier. The audio replay between my ears was deafening. Over and over her tattered voice dictated the words of a discombobulated mind and it enraged me as much as it broke my heart. This is what had shaped my mother.

To exacerbate my anger, I received several messages from my half-brother's new girlfriend stating that I was disgusting and that I should be ashamed of myself. I didn't point out the irony that at 24, she had more children than IQ points and collected a welfare cheque claiming them as dependents while latching on to my brother's meager income to support her habits. I blocked her, unsure of why she ever had my contact information in the first place.

I snuck out of work the next day on a sushi run for the Executive Producer to try to get in a few last words with my grandpa. I had no idea what to expect, but I hoped that either my grandma wouldn't be there or that tempers would have subsided. Neither was true; my grandma *and* my aunt stood outside his door like guards armed with vitriol and insidious hatred for me, the outsider. My grandma started in on me again, while her daughter looked on disdainfully from beneath her bushy black eyebrows. I scooted past to kiss Grandpa on the cheek.

"I love you." I said, through the lump in my throat.

"Can someone empty this tray of piss?" he pleaded, his eyes searching for a nurse.

He died the following Sunday, four days later. He'd made it to 90 in spite of drinking heavily for at least 80 of those years. He liked to boast of having his first drink at 8, when he'd rummage through the bushes at the local dance hall where party-goers would stash their moonshine. He wore his alcoholism like a badge of honor, as though how much he could drink made him more of a man instead of a glaring vulnerability that often had him in drunken tears half way through his daily 26er of gin at 2pm.

My ostracism from the family was swift. I got one message that he had died and that was it. It was like this was what they had been waiting for. All the judgement and hatred for my mom had been transferred to me and what she must've felt tenfold as an addict was enough to nearly knock me out. No wonder she'd needed heroin and booze and everything else she could hurl into her bloodstream to numb their malice. The dysfunction was a cyanide soup, each one of them their own hideous ingredient. I was fortunate to have been shunned, though I didn't feel fortunate. I felt sad and alienated, vengeful and enraged—except for when I was with Ben.

Ben was my protection blanket of inside jokes, shared food and day trips to cute little towns with goats on the roof and delicious tacos. I tried to think about work as much as I could, but it was just a joe job with a fancy title. Instead, I threw my passion into the new relationship. I gave him every bit of love that I wasn't getting, spoiling him with affection and ignoring every sign that he wasn't capable of being on the receiving end of it. He wanted to smoke weed with the friends he'd had since high school and dream about being a rock star while he tinkered away at the music studio he'd built in a town of 600 and I just wanted to be by his side because it felt warm and friendly there.

I went back to the city when the job ended and Ben broke up with me, citing that he didn't see a future for us. I couldn't see a future without him. It hit me hard, since all of my love was poured into him. I should've diversified.

Two Christmases and two birthdays passed and more nieces and nephews were born as reported by social media. The only communication I received was notice that I had been taken out of the will in one final slash at my well-being.

Ben and I text sometimes, but I need too much and maybe it makes him feel like a failure unable to give it. If everything was different though, it would've been perfect.

Feral Femme

We are so unimaginative about where we hide the key, any idiot could get in. Fortunately, there aren't many idiots in this neighborhood; a privilege we pay handsomely for. Property taxes nearly doubled last year, but it's not something worth fretting over. Make money, spend money, no matter; there's always more. Last I checked, the aging trophy wives with workaholic, alcoholic husbands and entitled teens whose mothers traded caring expressions for Botoxed foreheads would still need someone to listen to them unload for $350 an hour. And of course David's plays are in such high demand since the one with that movie star, he could hardly write them fast enough. What was that big star's name? It was a location, not an actual name. Dallas? Dakota?

David gets annoyed that I can't keep up with his work, but I've got too much on my mind to invest mental real estate in the talent. Maybe I'm a bad wife.

The gardener isn't keeping up with the jasmine. He needs to pluck the flowers as soon as they start to wilt before they fall to the ground. Otherwise, the bushes will stop blooming and I do so love to smell those fragrant white stars through the screen as I'm drifting off to sleep in the evening. I will remind him once more, but then I will have to start looking for a replacement.

I pad quietly into the kitchen and open the fridge where Matilda's school picture stares back at me. She looks so much like David I sometimes doubt I contributed any genes, but I love those serious brown eyes and the distinctive cowlick on the both of them. I chug a green juice from the door without bothering to get a glass, pausing to read the ingredients when my initial thirst is quenched. Blah, blah, blah, spirulina, turmeric, wheat grass. I doubt there is a difference between wheat grass and our lawn, but money in the bank makes us prone to falling for this kind of scam.

David won't be home for days and with Matilda at school in Switzerland this semester, I've got the house to myself this week. I shove sliced turkey into my mouth and eye the cinnamon buns Gabby baked in spite of my insistence that we keep carbs to a minimum.

Sinking into the leather couch, I wipe the turkey slime from my fingers on its arm. It gives it character and Gabby will be here to clean in the morning anyway. Some of our friends think it's unnecessary for us to have her every day, especially now that Matilda is away, but she's been with us for years and I don't like to cut back on anyone's employment. If someone wants to work, that should be their right. There are so many unemployed bums these days. Sitting outside the office, pan handling with some sob story. Always the same. Never making an effort to improve themselves or their lives. That could have just as easily been me, but I pulled myself up by the bootstraps because I'm better than that.

Feeling the chill of the sun going down, I head to the bedroom for a cardigan, but end up in the study instead. It was a long day. I'm glad to be nearing retirement when I will no longer need to repress my desire to scream obscenities about how entitled and spoiled the people I deal with are.

I slip off my shoes and retrieve the slippers from under the bed. They are too tight and I wonder if my feet are growing. They haven't done that since I was pregnant.

When my own mother got pregnant, my dad hit the road. He didn't want her to get fat; that's what she said, but who knows what's true.

Davey and I were 13 when we met. His voice was cracking, and I remember thinking how cute it was when he asked me to the sock-hop—that's what we called dances back then. Nowadays the kids don't even have dances. Too bad; they were such fun. I worry that Matilda is too studious as she looks back at me from another photograph in her rigid school uniform.

Davey's father and mother were married and didn't yell at each other, unless it was during a badminton match. He had two older sisters that would give me the clothes they didn't want anymore, and I'd pretend they were my sisters too. My mom never said no to my spending time there, since it meant she didn't have to feed me. That's probably why she called me chubby too.

Davey was sweet, his big brown eyes full of understanding when I didn't want to talk. I rarely went home, but when I was 15, I popped by our basement suite with 3 Skör bars and a bouquet of pink Gerber daisies for my mom's birthday.

Her head hung off the edge of the couch at an awkward angle. I tried to lift it onto the pillow, but her neck was stiff like a doll and the vomit in her hair had hardened. The coffee table told the same old story with a syringe and a spoon, the ashtray overflowing. The belt she said was my dad's, lay slack at her elbow.

Therapists say I disassociated that day, but that sounds like something they learned in a book of mumbo jumbo. What I really did was get to work. I put my dad's belt around my waist and I shoved the plastic baggie of brown dust into my bra. I cleaned out the bathroom cabinet full of all her 'medicine' and took everything else of value out of the apartment before calling 9-1-1. I walked back to Davey's while the paramedics were fussing with my mother's corpse.

When I laid in his arms that night I felt like a pail of cold water, unsure of where my edges were and who I was without a parent. I told him to have sex with me. It was our first time. I liked the sharpness of the pain as he jabbed away at me and I wanted more of it. I told him to put his hands around my neck the way I'd seen one of my mother's boyfriends do before I was old enough to talk.

"Squeeze tighter!" I squeaked.

"I don't want to hurt you, though."

"Don't be a little bitch."

Within weeks the ass smacking and hair pulling escalated to punching me in the stomach and biting 'til I bled.

"Harder! You hit like a girl!" I'd taunt him until his rage at being emasculated was beyond my control. Each time we took degradation a step further, but he couldn't match the hurt inside of me. I didn't want to be near him under any other circumstances and he could feel it, so he played my game. No one knew but us.

I overheard girls at school talk about their boyfriends and having to deal with an unwanted boner now and then when they were having their backs tickled during a movie in the rumpus room. I hid my bruises and felt outside of everything with my calcified heart.

I asked him to stop once, but he thought it was part of it. He was going to kill me if we kept that pace and funny, I didn't want to die.

I started selling my mom's pills to some of the dirtball kids and I took that money and bought more and within a few months I had a pretty good business. I rented the laundry room in an old lady's house close to the school and cut ties with Davey.

I started saving for college. It was something I heard other people were doing and with the help of a counselor, I applied for schools that were far away and a bunch of orphan scholarships.

Davey slid notes in my locker telling me I looked pretty or that he missed me. I crumpled them and went to class.

One night at an obnoxiously crowded party where I was making a ton of money selling Quaaludes and LSD out of one of the back bedrooms, he came in with a look on his face that begged for another chance. I wasn't expecting to see him amongst this drug-addled crowd, and it caught me totally off guard.

"What are you doing here?" I asked in a voice I barely recognized.

His smooth skin and tanned athletic arms were a welcome contrast to the pockmarked faces and scrawny bodies that had been desperately cycling through this grungy bedroom for the past few hours. His presence made them nervous enough to flee as fast as their high little legs would carry them and then we were alone.

"You can't do this," he said, barely above a whisper. "It's dangerous and it's beneath you."

My heart cracked open for a moment and it was a relief to let it. "You don't know what you're talking about," I said quietly. "Maybe I'm saving for school. Maybe I'll be a psychologist or even a doctor someday."

"I know you better than anyone, Puppy."

And there was something about feeling known that made me unable to resist when he kissed me softly and safely.

He got up to lock the door, laid me on a pile of coats and penetrated me in a way that made us feel new.

Unhinged by the intimacy, I decided to stay when he said he had to get home for curfew. He wasn't happy about it, but I wanted to know my edges.

"Are you sure, Lita? *This* is your choice?" His tone was laughably dramatic, and I didn't realize at the time that that choice was such a memorable one.

Twenty minutes later, there was a knock at the door; a loud, authoritative knock, much like the one I was hearing now.

"Hello?"

"Police!"

One of those silly actors stopping by unannounced no doubt. Why did David give out our goddamn address? Why did he need to be liked so much? God, his fear of rejection was still sickening after all these years.

Ugh, I'm going to ignore them. I want to take a bath and unwind with a nice glass of Rosé or maybe I'm more in the mood for a Sauvignon Blanc. Yes, but not too dry. That one the Hansen's brought over for card night was too dry. Probably gave it to us because they didn't want it. That would be so typical of Annette.

Bang! Bang! Bang! on the door. I dive behind the couch as four policemen come in with their weapons drawn.

I scream and they come running over with their shoes still on and no manners at all.

"Ma'am you're under arrest for breaking and entering, trespassing and destruction of property."

I shouldn't have wiped my hands on the expensive looking couch.

"Are you alone?" the young one barked in my ear as his lady partner patted me down.

"Do you have anything that's going to poke me, ma'am? Any needles or sharp objects?"

"Of course not!"

I can hear the murmur of some nosy neighbor asking questions and an officer answering calmly while another one rudely slaps handcuffs on me.

"No no, nothing to worry about," said the police lady.

Murmur, murmur, murmur, replied the nosy bitch.

"Yes, we're thankful you called. We've notified the homeowner, apparently he's in New York directing a play.

Murmur, murmur.

"Thinks she lives here...."

They put me in handcuffs. They're too tight. This is an outrage.

A Helping Hand

It's 8:20 a.m. and I'm putting out the ketchup and jam for our breakfast rush. Faye follows behind me with napkins and cutlery, setting the tables efficiently, her long auburn pony tail swishing behind her.

Grant sits in the corner, pouring gin from his Thermos into the plastic cup that accompanies it. I don't need to look to know that his hand shakes unsteadily, but still he does not spill a precious drop.

He will drink deliberately at first, his eyelids closed with relief and then, as it spills into his thirsty bloodstream, his hands will shake a little less and he will gain gusto, so that by ten, while Faye and I call out omelet orders and drop off extra syrup, he will be swigging like it's an Olympic event.

When we bought this place and built the lovely suite upstairs, I planned to spend my free time luxuriating in novels and bubble baths and gazing at the lake for hours on end enjoying the peace, but there is no peace in close proximity to a drunk, so I find my joy in this kitchen where delight tickles my fingertips as I carefully shape pastry leaves for the tops of rhubarb, peach and huckleberry pies and the smell of freshly baked bread replaces the syrupy stench that Grant sweats profusely.

I sometimes wonder if living above the restaurant contributed to his sickness. Maybe if his commute were longer he'd be more responsible or maybe he'd have driven his car off a steep embankment never to be heard from again. Maybe then the kids would come round.

As I hear him buffalo-thump up the stairs, I lock the front door, but not the back because when the breeze decides to bless us, there is no denying the goodness of being alive.

A Helping Hand

I put my apron on and pull out flour, sugar, almond paste, chocolate chips and butter from the fridge.

I turn Patsy Cline as loud as the speakers will allow, sway my hips and sing. My chocolate croissants are something to sing about.

Grant is the real musician in our family. Well, he was. There was a time when there seemed nothing he couldn't do. Both my sisters had crushes on him, but it was me he asked out, and I wasn't about to say no since my sister's crushes never lasted long.

He had these eyes. Soulful, tortured eyes that spun me around at a dizzying pace but caught me softly before I lost my balance. When he spoke, my body relaxed, and I sighed contentedly so often that my sisters started to make fun, imitating me every chance they got and asking what my wedding colors were going to be.

"She's going to do Dusty Rose—you know she is. Pink has always been Lyssie's favorite color," squeaked Lila. "And long gloves, no doubt! I'll look so elegant in long gloves, don't you think?" She held out her arms, wiggling her fingers and giggling.

Pippa chimed in, having been planning her own wedding since she was about seven.

"What about green, Elyse? To match your eyes? Or*rrr*" ...she gasped, "burgundy! I saw in one of them magazines at the drug store this bridal party in head-to-toe burgundy and they looked posh as all get out! I'll bet if you do burgundy you'll get the front page of the wedding section."

"The paper's in black and white; no one will know what color the dresses are," I said, trying to hide how thrilled I was at the idea.

"But the photographer'll know, and she'll wanna print the poshest picture she can to keep up with, ya know, fashion."

Mama came in, her gardening gloves full of sweet peas. "What are y'all so excited about?"

"Elyse has found the one! Grant is her Prince Charming, isn't he Lyssie?! She's so happy Mama, all she does is sigh and walk around here like she's countin' the minutes 'til she gets to go on another date."

"Well, we all love Grant, but there's no need to rush, is there Lyssie-baby? You've been dating what, six weeks?"

"Sometimes you just know," whispered Pippa with a wink.

They were right of course. I did know and we did get married, but just to be my own person I chose sunshine yellow for their dresses and big yellow hats with daisies that matched their bouquets. It was a happy color and that's how I felt with him and about the wonderful future than lay before us at 18 and 21-years-old.

I had the world by the tail those first couple of years. He was the life of the party and by association it made me fun and socially sought after. We were always off to somewhere. Picnics with friends, tipsy moonlit skinny-dips, dancing to live bands at the hall, or him at the piano after supper at my parent's with everyone singing along, gin gimlets and homemade beers in hand.

We had Caroline, then Colin and before I knew it, Colleen. It was whirlwind of baby-making and then raising those babies and though they were my everything, it sure took it outta me. My body wasn't my own. Someone was either in my belly or wanting theirs filled. I was Grant's wife and mother of three. When he'd reach for me at night, I didn't have a drop left to give and the thought of him putting another baby put me left me sour. I had to sit some the parties out, at first claiming my sisters and Mama were too busy to watch the kids, but eventually admitting I was too exhausted. Ten years in I still loved him, but not with any of the zest I once had. Mama told me that was natural.

Grant got lonesome and I suppose that was my fault. I made an effort when I could, listening to his voice bellow story after repeated story as I laughed politely instead of focusing on the spittle gathering in the corners of his mouth.

When the girls went off to college, I was left with Colin, who was kind as a Labrador and helpful around the house, but had no ambition to leave and since I felt I'd done enough full-time mothering, I started looking at businesses. Grant liked the idea too. We saw a car wash, two laundromats, a pet shop and a few restaurants before settlin' on Gabby's. It had a real nice feel and I figured we could have ourselves a nice family business. Grant's impending retirement only made it seem like a better idea since the alternative was him having more time to drink like a damned fish.

Gabby's was a breakfast spot with a loyal clientele and Gabby herself was as sweet as pecan pie. Every detail was meticulous, from the eyelet curtains she'd sewn herself to the hand-painted signs for the bathrooms.

She walked us through every aspect of the business—from the recipes, to the customers, to what to do when the wasps tried to build their nest out back. I liked her and I wished she could stay, but her plans to travel sounded much more glamorous and a pang of envy squeezed my heart.

It wasn't long before Colin set out on a missionary expedition to South Africa. I cried for three days even though I knew it was time for him to spread his wings and for me to find mine. We got postcards with pictures of the mud huts he was building and wildlife like we'd only ever seen on television. Caroline kept us close with pictures of the kids and lots of phone calls, while

Colleen consecutively made the Dean's List and was always up for some award or another, but they didn't visit, and we all knew why.

Grant was doing well for a while, when we were busy getting going. He kept the liquor upstairs and got chummy with our cooks tasting things and making suggestions here and there. He was very likable without the drink.

It was nice then. Nice to have something in common and I thought maybe we'd get to know each other again, but it didn't go that way. Grandma used to always say, if you want to make God laugh, tell him your plans.

When he coached the contractor on what it was I wanted our bathroom to look like with the skylight overhead and the step up to the bathtub, I remembered what it was like to feel respect for him, until he asked the contractor and his wife for dinner and drank so much he nodded off before we'd finished our salads. I was left to apologize and try to hold a conversation with two sympathetic but judgmental strangers. I was livid.

A Helping Hand

Waking up to the piss-soaked recliner didn't make things any better.

Pity, anger and guilt dominated my life.

Pity because he was obviously not well. Anger because our lives might have been so beautiful, and I might have done so many things if I wasn't saddled with him. Every moment he was out drinking, or in drinking, and I was wiping runny noses, cleaning endless dishes and trudging through the multiplication tables, were moments of my life I would never get back and I seethed about them as the years went by and grey hairs sprouted on my head. And guilt for how disgusted I felt when he wanted to make love and for feeling so much rage at a man whom I had vowed to love in sickness and in health.

I lived in fear, but I could never put my finger on what the fear was. There were so many. He might fall and split his fat head open or hurt one of the kids by accident or drive over someone with his car. He passed out cold on one of our pups once and suffocated him. I had to bury his snuggly little body in the back yard before the girls woke up, lie to them about what had happened, and then comfort them while they sobbed. I hated him for that.

Nothing was safe.

After Colin left, I hired Faye—one of the best things I've ever done. She lived three streets over with her daughter who had recently started grade one. I didn't like to pry, but there was no man in the picture, and she didn't seem to mind one bit. She was peppy and always showed up with a smile and clean sneakers. The customers loved her and I did too. I didn't realize how much I'd needed a friend until I had one.

On the days she didn't have to pick up her little one from school, we'd chat for hours. We got to be close as kittens over the next few months and still she never mentioned the child's father. I figured she didn't want to talk about it and I understood as Grant's half-closed eyes bore into us from his corner while we sipped our tea.

****

It's a Tuesday morning in October. The air is crisp and the sun bounces off the mosaic tables making everything seem bright and worth living for.

A Helping Hand

Faye brought me a beautiful bouquet of Dahlias from her garden, and I've been thinking about which vase would suit them best all morning. I decide on an old-fashioned lemonade jug that has been in our family for years as I pull them out of the fridge.

The oven is preheating for the croissants, and I am loving this 'me time' as they call it in the magazines.

I smell Grant's rotting liver before I turn 'round and see him. He's standing in just his button-down shirt and socks.

"Oh, Darling, you startled me!"

He smiles his lopsided grin.

"Where in the heck are your pants? You don't want someone seeing you like that! The curtains are just for show. They don't hide a thing. C'mon, let's get you upstairs."

I take his forearm and try to turn him back toward the stairs, but he stands like an ox.

He reaches for my left breast, kneading it like dough.

I shriek, an unrecognizable sound.

He grumbles something incoherent and his breath hits me in a vile brown cloud.

"C'mon now, let's get you a coffee."

"No coffee, I want my wife. You seen my wife?"

"I'm right here, but we can't have you down here with no pants. Now, c'mon, let's go upstairs."

"You won't come with me. I want my wife. I want…"

He starts to cry.

"Oh, Grant, come on now. Don't be silly."

He pushes his weight into me and leans his head on my shoulder. I turn mine as I feel my buttocks press into the countertop. He pulls at my yellow dress with no comprehension that the zipper is in the back, and he will get nowhere tugging at it like a child.

His face so close to mine makes me want to vomit. I focus on the flowers. Pinks, deep purples and a yellow one that peeks up above the others, seeing everything.

"Please?" he begs, his swollen red nose wet with mucus.

A Helping Hand

My mind races for an excuse. Something reasonable. Something he can comprehend in this state.

"The door is open, someone could, Grant, let me--"

He lifts me on to the counter bumping my head against the cupboard. I search for a prayer, but nothing comes. As far as I get is "Dear God, dear God, dear God as he enters me with his pathetic excuse for an erection. I am as dry as the flour on my hands and it hurts as he stiffens inside of me, but not as much as the fiery shame.

"You tell that dyke you're my wife. You're *my* wife."

But I wasn't. I'd left him years before he stood there, clobbering clumsily away at me.

One hundred years later, I hear the back door swing open and Faye's sing-song voice.

"Hey, doll, I left my apron with my tips in it! Gosh, I'd lose my head if it wasn't...." She comes around the corner and I think I say 'help', but I can't be sure because before I know it my dear God plea has been answered.

I hear the clang of pans and the familiar quick-paced footsteps of Faye's Keds before Grant falls like a bag of wet laundry to the floor.

I pull my dress down and my underpants up and I wipe my tears with my floury hand.

Faye takes me into her arms and holds me close like a mother baboon as I stare at the lemonade jug full of beautiful hand-picked flowers. Grant lays on the floor.

"Shoot, did I kill him?" Faye whispers.

"I hope so."

"I'll tell the police it was me. I'll tell the truth. I won't let you get in trouble." Her brown eyes are scared, but I see boundless love in them.

"I'd like to get out of here. Away from him. As far away from him as possible."

"Sure, yeah, let's go somewhere. What about this, though?" She points at my unconscious husband.

I watch him for a moment, fighting the urge to step on his throat. I watch his chest rise slightly. He's alive for now but who knows, maybe he won't make it up the stairs without me helping him along like a human cane.

A Helping Hand

"Let's let fate take its course."

I locked the back door and we got on our bikes and rode down to the lake. Faye lit a cigarette and I watched as the swirls of smoke danced around her pretty head.

"Would your kids miss their dad if he were gone? Would it break their hearts I mean?"

"My kids? Hard to say. They might be relieved. I know I would be. I might be going straight to hell for saying that aloud, but I don't care anymore. If he died they might come around again. I think about that sometimes."

Faye put her arm around my shoulder. She smelled like the earth and there was an unmistakable familiarity that grounded me and made my voice come from deeper within.

"I loved him once. A lot. It was that young love that sticks to you. There was never a day that I woke up and thought, 'I don't love my husband anymore.' I just carried on. Until today."

"You can leave."

"I'm not going anywhere. I've worked too hard to get Gabby's where it is. I like talking to folks, hearing about their days and bringing 'em a nice hot breakfast. I like waking up early, gettin' the ovens going, putting the sign out. I like feeding the squirrels yesterday's bread and sweepin' the sidewalk.

"It's the first thing I've had that's mine and I'll be damned if that drunk is going to take that from me too."

"What if he remembers what happened?"

"I'll tell him he deserved it."

I stayed at Faye's that night, in her daughter's bed, surrounded by stuffed animals. I got up at four, like always, and snuck over to the restaurant for business as usual.

I could hear Grant snoring as I showered and dressed. He had made it as far as the couch, still in his dress shirt and nothing else. Ordinarily I would have covered him up and given him a cup of hot coffee, but not today. I opened the windows, to let the air in, not caring if he caught a chill. He was his own problem now.

A Helping Hand

He came down later than usual and more bedraggled, but with his Thermos in hand, of course.

Faye brought him a plate of waffles and bacon.

"Thanks, hon," he mumbled politely, either not remembering she'd belted him with a cast iron frying pan less than 24-hours earlier, or scared into submission.

Later at the dish pit, I noticed she had his Thermos. "How on earth did you pry that out of his grip?" I asked in awe.

"I replaced it with another. Now he's got two."

I rolled my eyes. "Just what he needs. More to drink."

"This one is a new blend. He won't taste the difference though."

We held eyes for a long moment before the ding of the kitchen bell let us know an order was up.

I took the plates. Two on my left arm and one in my right hand. I was getting good at this, but I couldn't quite get the plate of toast. Faye had my back though.

"Faye, honey could you grab the--"

"I'm on it!" she smiled her bright, loyal smile.

Eleven Days 'til Sunday

The straps of my duffel bag take turns falling off my shoulder and my backpack is relentless in its efforts to tip me. After several sweaty minutes, I make it to the hallway where once cream-colored paint has turned grey, save for the stains splattered and sprayed every which way.

Some of the doors have numbers. Some don't. 307 does, though the seven is drawn on with a marker. This is my room for the week and I force the key into the shaky lock, near a snap of rage when it swings open and an exceptionally bony girl covered in tattoos stands in front of me.

"Hey, I'm Kimmie."

"Oh, hey."

I get all of my miserable crap inside the room and ditch what I can on the bed Kimmie doesn't appear to be using.

"You work today?" I ask.

"Yeah, there's no one down there."

"You live here?"

"Nah, Campbell River. Me an' my ol' man got into a scrap and I had to get out the house. Didn't tell him where I was going. Let 'im tweak a little, ya know?"

The room smells of her cheap body spray, the sulfur of matches burned in the bathroom and 80+ years of whatever else has gone wrong here.

"How long you been dancin'?" she asks in a sandpapery voice.

"I started at The Lion's Den last week and now here."

"A rookie, eh? I'm surprised Randy sent you here."

"Why?"

She shrugs. "They usually send you to the nice places first. Make ya think it's all glamorous or somethin'."

"He needed a fill in. Said he'd owe me a favor."

"Yeah, Caramel Sunday didn't show up. Knowing her she g-holed or overdosed or some shit. Hey, where are you next week?"

"I'm here for two weeks. Well, eleven days now since it's already Wednesday."

"You doin' the island tour?"

"Uh-huh. Campbell River next week."

She scoffs like I've said the wrong thing even though I am trying so hard not to. "If you see my ol' man at JJ's tell him he's a fuckin' goof, alright?!"

I nod, a little frightened of the change in her mostly cordial tone.

"You know 'im? Mike? Beard? Rides a silver Panhead?"

"No, nuh-uh. Don't know any Mikes."

She looks at me suspiciously, as though I might be the problem between she and bearded Mike.

157.

"You have to cover your tattoos to work here?" I ask. We need to move on from Mike.

She laughs. "Nobody's lookin' at my arms and legs. They don't care none 'bout some ink."

"Can we open a window?"

"Good idea. I need a smoke."

She lights a cigarette and yanks upward on the window that looks out onto the snow covered roof-top. It doesn't budge and the room starts to fill with smoke. I try not to cough as I join the effort, pulling as hard as I can on the two metal handles, but its painted shut. It is the only spot in the entire building that has seen a fresh coat of paint since it was built. What luck.

"Do we have a schedule yet?"

"Yeah, it's on the mirror. It goes me, then you, then me, then you extretera, extretera."

The mirror has several lipstick prints on it and I wonder about the girls that have come before me and why they felt okay about putting their lips on such a revolting surface.

I'm on stage at noon tomorrow, then three, six and nine pm et cetera, et cetera.

I hang my costumes as best I can from the bent metal hangers in the closet and take a shower that leaves me feeling like I am becoming one with this room and like the only difference between Kimmie and I are tattoos and poor diction.

It's snowing again. Small, hard pellets hit my windshield as I drive into town and go through the Wendy's drive-thru. I sit in the parking lot wondering what my grandma would think if she knew I was so close by. Maybe I'll spend the day with her before I drive to the next shit hole. I'll lie to her about what I'm doing. I'll let her think I'm a receptionist at the gym working my way up to $14 an hour and free aerobics classes and she'll believe me because she can hardly remember my name.

When I get back to the room, Kimmie is smoking cocaine from a piece of tin foil. She swears each time she burns her thumb on the spark wheel of her yellow lighter. I'm grateful that she doesn't notice me come in as I lay down with all my clothes on, careful not to let my skin touch anything. Through the thin walls, I can hear a loose, phlegmy cough.

I wake the next morning to Kimmie's guttural snore and think about the filthy state of a windpipe that emits such vile sounds.

There is no one in the bar when I arrive for my first show. A dozen or so tables are strewn about the room with folding metal chairs of various heights. One of them hosts a plate with some toast crusts and a few cold fries on it. Ants are spreading the word about it; however it is they do that, and I watch them scurry and scuttle, thrilled with their find. There's a neon Budweiser sign on the fritz and it flashes and pops, its tinny hum the only sound in the place.

I give my tape to the bartender and she looks me up and down in my red sequined dress, far too posh for an empty bar in a town of millworkers and fishermen and I feel apologetic for it even though the costumes are my favorite part of this whole endeavor. Nowhere else in my life do I have the occasion to wear sequins, lace gloves, or hot pink PVC. With each elaborate getup comes the accompaniment of my new alter ego, Desiree Brooks. Desiree is confident, daring and nearly 6 inches taller in her stilettos. She thinks that stripping is the kind of career that might make her interesting and that all the men who desire her will make up for the one that left when she was a baby.

"We gotta wait 'til at least three people in the bar before I put choo on," crowed the frumpy barmaid.

"Sure."

"You take a seat here and I'll give you the wave when it's time."

I plunk down on the swivel stool with my blanket in my lap and look around.

Posters of my predecessors hang on the wall, their autographed butts in the air and pumped-up tits showing through trashy school girl uniforms and faux nurse's attire. When I got my tonsils out, I don't remember any nurses in white satin mini-dresses or tiny paper hats adorned with red crosses, but a stripper's interpretation of reality varies a lot from a civilian's.

A man with a thin combover and no front teeth shuffles up to the bar in house slippers. Without saying anything the barmaid slides a coffee across the counter and plunks three sugar cubes in it and a shot of whiskey beside, while he fumbles for some change.

He turns his unshaven face to me. "You the stripper?"

I nod, feeling exposed by the rhetorical question.

"I'm Arvin." He shuffles into the darkness until I can barely make out his gargoyle-like silhouette at a corner table.

Twenty minutes later a group of three come. Two of them sidle up to front row while the third goes to the bar and gets a pitcher of beer. He looks me over and I try to be Desiree.

"Hi." I squeak baring my teeth in what I mean to be a smile.

He tips his greasy baseball hat and nods, "Hey, darlin'."

I hear my song come on and the bartender wags her finger in my direction.

I strut across the stage, begging my ankles not to give way as I make my way to the pole.

Desiree takes over. She wiggles and jiggles, twists and spreads and listens to the music instead of the lewd commentary from the men just inches from her naked vagina.

The one with the goatee is especially attentive. She can't see his eyes, but she knows they're on her and she likes that he's interested, even if it is for the wrong reasons.

She slides her naked back down the pole, kicking one leg way up and steadying herself with the other. She is still working on this move and hits the floor with her tailbone harder than she would like. She grimaces through the pain and Arvin winces when he hears the thud from his seat in the corner though she can't see him.

Goatee puts a five-dollar bill on the stage and she personalizes the show for him, bending over and spreading her labia with her manicured nails. The nails still feel awkward. She can't do up her jeans or pick up change if a cashier puts it on the counter, but they're part of the image she now adheres to.

Her last song stops abruptly and she hopes that the ghetto blaster hasn't chewed up her tape as she picks up her fuzzy blanket and wraps it around her nakedness, tucking it securely under her armpits. She bends to pick up her tip and Goatee speaks.

"You wanna come join us for a drink, hon'?"

She doesn't have a response ready for this yet.

"Oh, um, sure."

Upstairs Kimmie is frantically throwing costumes around apparently looking for something. "You seen my Mötley Crüe set?" she barks accusingly.

"Your music?"

She stares at me long enough to be uncomfortable. "Never mind, I think I left it in my truck. Who's down there?"

"I dunno, like three guys in the front and some guy named Arvin."

"He was in a bad accident and everyone died, Irene said."

"Who's Irene?"

"Oh, fuck yeah! Here's my tape! Right on, man I always dance to my Crüe first set." She slams the door behind her and I hear her clomp down the stairs like a Clydesdale. There's over an hour 'til her show, but maybe she can't tell time.

I'm not sure what to wear back down to the bar. Are those guys expecting Desiree? I have to get these shoes off my feet, so I put on my real clothes and my real

Eleven Days 'til Sunday

shoes and feel real weird when I greet Goatee and his friends with excruciatingly dirty fingernails. They are machinists and I don't care what that means, but I know I never want a finger that dirty inside of me.

We sit and drink. I have three vodka cranberries and a shot of Jameson. We seem to be in celebratory mode now, maybe because we're getting along so well and they're so attentive. Roy, the only name I can remember because I have an uncle called that, is giving me a foot rub and I almost fall asleep because it feels so good and my feet are so tired of being crammed into those silly heels. Small town guys are really nice.

I'm jolted awake when Kimmie comes on stage singing loudly to her rock music and yelling with a force usually reserved for someone trying to save her child from being hit by a bus.

"Clap you motherfuckers! You wanna see these titties or what?!"

No wonder her wind pipe is so thrashed.

My new friends clap and whistle and Goatee stands up and lifts his shirt, dancing like a buffoon. Halfway through her first song it's like I no longer exist to them. Roy has abandoned the massage and I put my shoes back on and sit up as straight as I can. I stand, hoping one of them will notice, but I slip out the fire exit without a nod.

The air smacks me boldly from my sloppiness and I feel tears in my eyes. It's hard to decipher what they are for.

There's a pay phone across the parking lot and I think about calling someone, but who? I walk over anyway, wanting a purpose. I step inside the booth and lean against the glass, pushing my head against its cold. I pick up the receiver and push the buttons, listening to the beeps and boops they make in my ear. The reality makes me ache.

Across the lot I see Roy and Goatee come out and light cigarettes. I turn my back to them and the phone utters a cacophony of warnings for me to hang up if I'm not actually serious about making a call. I put down the receiver and see Roy making his way over as Goatee's back is swallowed by the door and he returns to the bar.

Roy and I sit on the curb and smoke. I just hold mine because it makes me sick. I can smell his breath and

I'm aware that he's too close to me, but it's okay until it suddenly isn't.

I stand up. "I've got a show soon. I should go get ready."

"Nah, there's no one in there."

"Really? I hope they don't cancel it. I don't get paid if it's canceled."

"I'll pay ya to sit out here with me."

"I'm freezing."

"Yeah, it's cold as a witch's tit. I'll go warm up my truck and we can hang out in there."

I'm sobering up. "I'm just gonna go inside, maybe get something to eat. I haven't eaten anything yet today."

He pulls a chocolate bar out of his flannel pocket. "You like Mars bars?"

I eat it in 3 or 4 very grateful bites, feeling a peanut fall in my lap, but chewing too voraciously to stop and pick it up.

Roy laughs, revealing a gold-outlined eye tooth. "You need someone to take care of you, don't you?"

"I should get back." I stand to walk, less wobbly now, energized by the sugar.

I'm almost to the door when he grabs my wrist.

"Hey, don't go yet." His nose is red and its blackheads make him the ugliest man in the world.

"I'll see you later. Thanks for the chocolate."

"Oh, so it's like that, eh? Let me buy ya drinks, smoke my smokes, eat my food, lead me on and then take off?"

"I don't even smoke."

I am about 3 feet from the door when I see it rock a little and then open slowly as if the person on the other side has the strength of a newly born fawn. Arvin the guy that drinks whiskey with his coffee, hunches over, trying to light his pipe.

"Marvin!" I shout far too loudly.

He nods, politely, without correcting me.

"You gonna go use him now then?" Roy hisses.

I walk toward Arvin and fall into him when I trip over the curb. He catches me and we sway like saplings in a windstorm. I hold onto his neck, feeling its warmth and the softness of the downy hair that still clings to his head. His arms are around my waist I think, and we steady each other after 20 precarious seconds in which we might both tumble to the ground. At first all I can hear is Roy's steel-toed boots staggering away, as he mutters words like *bitch* and *freeloader*, but when he is gone, there are breathy sobs, teeth chattering and noses sucking back snot and whose sounds are whose doesn't matter. Arvin and I stand in each other's arms crying hard for a good long while before I untangle myself and hear him say softly, "Sorry."

I climb the stairs two at a time wanting to get away quickly and quietly like a jaguar. I wipe dripping mascara from my face and watch my spray tan streak across the back of my hand.

Kimmie is smoking from her tin foil again.

"Did nobody tell ya it's bad fuckin' manners to sit in gyno when another broad's on stage?"

"What?"

"Don't be such an attention whore. You get your eighteen minutes on stage."

"Sorry."

"Have you been crying?"

"No, I'm good."

"It's alright. I'm just trying to look out for you. Some chicks get pissed about that shit."

By Friday I know that I have to be Desiree in all my interactions. With Kimmie, with the men in the bar, with the bartenders that try to get me to wait for them to finish their phone calls before they put me on stage.

"Hey, it's 2:05," I bark, pointing at my watch letting them know that I'm the fucking priority.

After listening to her call him a limp dick cocksucker and a piece of shit loser, for three days Kimmie decides to leave early and go back to Mike.

"I'm sure he's pretty horny by now, he'll treat me right for a few days."

"You'd leave me here?"

She looks right through me like she's never seen me before.

Mike comes to pick her up after her first show and I am left alone in the room.

By Monday the rancidity seeping in from the hallway makes me miss the smell of her body spray and charbroiled drugs.

I'm the only dancer here now and while the agents try to find a replacement, I have to do shows every hour and a half instead of every three. There isn't much turnover in the crowd, and they are as sick of me as I am of them. I have to repeat costumes and my back aches from arching it. Thank God, I haven't seen Arvin or Roy again though. I wouldn't know how to act.

After the voices underneath my window quiet down that night and the floor stops shaking from the music, a silence seeps into my bones and hangs out there like a pack of teenagers loitering in a food court. I miss everyone I can think of and people I've never met.

The bed creaks under my weight as I let out a breath I hadn't realized I was holding. I think about smashing a pane of the window to get some air in here, but I worry I will freeze solid and someone will have to tell my grandma what I'm doing in a place like this.

Sunday I only have four shows since even the degenerates that hang out in strip clubs all day have families to be with. I'm too tired to do much and I wish I could just watch TV, but this place is getting to me, so I go to the Tim Horton's between shows and play solitaire and drink black coffee because it seems edgier than cream and sugar.

When I get back, the hallway still smells like rotting garbage and the contrast of the coffee and donut break I've just given my nose makes it less tolerable. I burn the incense I tucked in the front pocket of my suitcase and tuck a dirty towel under the door to fill the gap.

When I come down for my last show on Friday night Irene is talking to the cook. I hear Arvin's name, but I can't tell what they're saying with the hockey game playing loudly on the radio. Maybe they know why he was crying last week. Maybe that's why he hasn't been back.

I mention the stink upstairs, but she doesn't care.

I finish yet another strip show mirroring the lack of enthusiasm from the men that have seen my naked body nearly as many times as their spouse's by now. I jog up the stairs to get into my room as fast as I can and twist my ankle hearing myself screech in pain. The gasp of air I involuntarily suck in is so foul I gag as I hobble to 307.

I fall asleep at some point and awaken to heavy footsteps, walkie talkies and the snapping of a stretcher being assembled. I get dressed and stick my head into the hallway to see a black bag being wheeled by and a man with a jacket that says *Coroner* on the back.

I cover my mouth, feeling the contents of my stomach push between my fingers.

"You should go back inside ma'am," a clean-cut young fireman says professionally.

A lady in a uniform hands me a handful of tissues and a kidney bean shaped tray to throw up in. The rest of the crew move through the hallway and we are alone.

"I'm sorry about your neighbor," she says gently.

"I don't live here."

"Did you know him?"

"I don't know anyone."

She looks at me curiously.

"I mean I don't know anyone here. I'm just, I'm just here 'til Sunday."

"He's lived here a long time, but he liked his privacy apparently. Hotel will be shut down for contamination, I reckon. You have somewhere else to go?"

"Who was he?"

She looks inside her metal clipboard. "Arvin Livingston."

I fall back against the door, feeling the paint chips on the backs of my arms. Arvin.

"I did know him…he had a cough."

"I'm sorry."

She puts a warm hand on my forearm and I see eyes that feel sorry for me. I pull away, close the door and pack my things to move to the next town.

Madonna Whore

It's been over twenty years since I slept with a husband that wasn't my own, vowing never to let my heart get involved in something so messy again, but my heart is nowhere near this.

At first it gives me anxiety, but no worse than the paralysis of not knowing how I'm going to pay the rent or being $32 short for my electric bill. I've been through countless jobs and back to school several times, racking up debt along the way, but the weight of my inner world has become too heavy to put up with the indecencies of working for a living.

Having someone take an interest in me feels good, even if it is just sexual. He's flashy. Jersey Shore rich. Not my type, but I fool my body into thinking he is long enough to recalibrate the crippling depression of being dropped like a reeking trash bag by a struggling musician with a poetic vocabulary and beautiful hands. He said I was codependent; a word he'd learned from my replacement with her ironic glasses and facial piercings. She's a Vlogger. I'm a wreck.

Maybe the wife would understand since she snatched him from his previous one. Maybe we'd laugh about it, or perhaps she'd slit my jugular after publicly outing me as a home wrecking slut. Her profile told me she liked trips to Vegas with girl gangs who mirrored her fake eyelashes and silicone tits. They took pictures of themselves toasting Dom Perignon in very small dresses, their $5,000 handbags perched in front of their alcohol-bloated bellies. I've had the same purse for at least twelve years. I got it at a thrift store on the pier and I still get compliments on it, but not from women like them.

When I ask my therapist why men cheat, she brings up the Madonna Whore Complex and since his wife was an escort, I guess that makes me Madonna. I will consider this pious label more carefully next time I'm coming in his mouth.

One Thousand Dollars

I parked a couple of blocks away where it was free after ten. As I teetered up to the lights of the hotel in my highest heels, a salty breeze blew my hair back and I felt edgy and cool, like someone might make a movie about me.

The doorman smiled and graciously opened the glass door for me to slip through and I hoped no one and everyone saw me.

He looked like his picture. I was grateful, not because he was handsome, but because I was able to recognize him instantly, sparing me potential embarrassment. He recognized me too as he stood and smiled.

A suit-clad employee pulled out my chair and I thanked him, wanting to whisper that the tag was still on this dress and that I would return it tomorrow.

"I'm not this girl!" I shouted inside myself.

He took my hand and kissed it just as casually as someone else might shake it. "You are as breathtaking as your pictures."

Was I supposed to say the same?

"Would you like something to drink?" he asked.

As if the servers had bionic hearing, one was at our table before he got the final word out.

"I'll have an Amaretto Sour, please."

The waiter walked away and I wondered what the hell to talk about.

"Have you been here before?" he asked.

"No, it's lovely though."

"Yeah, it's got a mellow vibe."

My drink was deliciously sweet and tart and so was the next one and the two after that.

"I've never done this before." My skin felt hot. "I bet everyone says that right?"

He leaned in and said softly in my ear, "I believe you."

He seemed comfortable. Maybe he was attractive. "Can I be your first?" he asked taking my hand.

"It's a thousand dollars."

He nodded and got up to go to the cash machine. The waiter came by again. Had he heard us?

He was gone a long time and I reached for my phone—a video message from the babysitter of Sampson sleeping soundly in his crib. I felt a lump in my throat and chased it off by crunching an ice cube, hoping it might freeze my heart for the next hour.

The elevator was full of mirrors and when I saw my reflection from every angle I wondered if it was really me.

The room was stylish and hip, like it had been designed that week in the interest of staying current. The scent of dried eucalyptus emanated from vases so delicate they seemed to hover above the raw edged wooden tables. A couch as wide as my bed was stacked with fluffy pillows each with artistic designs and I wanted to spend twenty minutes appreciating each one of them, but I wasn't being paid for that.

He led me to the bedroom, with a luxurious four post bed surrounded by candles that had already been lit and smelled like lilacs and jasmine and the most romantic of smells. Was he wooing me? He sat on the bed and I stood in front of him, slipping my dress off my hips and letting it fall to the floor. I left my shoes and lingerie on because it seemed like something a professional would do. He unhooked my bra and I knelt before him, so he wouldn't see how much the undergarment had deceived him.

I gave him oral sex and then kneeled on the bed while he slipped into a condom and then me.

The duvet was a luxuriously high thread count and the downy pillows nicely cushioned my palms as I made noises that implied he was in charge.

His cock was big, but not too big and he kept a good pace as his hand moved up and down my back and squeezed my ass confidently. My body relaxed and fell into being turned on, as if it knew no difference between this man and one that wasn't paying for the privilege of my time.

He finished and dressed.

I started to dress too.

"You can keep the room," he said. "Order room service if you like."

He left 10 one-hundred-dollar bills on the dresser and quietly exited.

I thought about staying. Ordering lobster and chocolate truffles, but the room smelled more like sex than candles now and I wanted to go home and brush my cheek against my baby's head.

*****

His name was Mark. Just Mark. He was an architect. Lived in Brentwood. I assumed he was married by the ring he didn't bother to remove, but I wouldn't ask about that. With the money came his freedom from questions and my disinterest in asking them.

We met at the same hotel. The familiarity put me at ease and hopeful that the staff who recognized me would think that I was the one who had placed the ring on his finger in spite of my not baring my own. I silently willed them to think it was at the jewelers for a cleaning and that the next time we came I'd have a very shiny diamond as a symbol of my husband Mark's devotion to me.

"Amaretto Sour?" my make-believe husband asked me as the waiter neared.

I thought back to the hangover I'd nursed from the sugary drink, but I wouldn't need so many this time.

"Please."

The drinks arrived and Mark looked at me. Like, *really* looked at me.

"You're back."

"I enjoyed your company." I said, with a slight raise in my voice at the end, as though I might be asking a question, but not quite.

He smiled. "Did you?"

"I didn't not enjoy it."

"I like honesty. Thank you."

"Why are *you* back? I'm sure there are no shortage of options on those sites."

"There's something about you."

"What?"

"Hmmm, good question. An innocence?"

"This isn't innocent."

"No, so I guess I appreciate the honesty of that. When you said it was your first time it turned me on. I felt honored to be your 'first'."

"You want me to wear pigtails next time?"

He looked at me again. I'd gone too far. Shit.

"We're deciding on next time already?"

"No, I...was just kidding."

"You're funny."

"Why don't you laugh then?" His eyes laughed.

"My wife was my first, but I wasn't hers."

"Did you get married young?"

"Twenty-six."

"That's young."

"We were in love and we had been for so long at that point that there seemed no reason not to."

"And now?"

"And now, what?"

"Are you in love?"

"These are deep questions for a second date." "

"I'm sorry."

"Don't be. I like depth."

"Are we on a date? Is that what this is?"

"What would you call it?"

"A date is fine. I believe the correct term is arrangement though; according to the site, we were both seeking 'arrangements'."

"Do you believe in fate?" he asked.

"Yeah, sure."

"I believe that's what this is. Fate. That you and I met because we were meant to."

"Okay, *now* it feels like a date because you sound like you are trying to seduce me."

"Would it work? If I were?"

"The thousand bucks makes it a sure thing. We don't need to talk about the stars aligning and all that jazz."

He laughed. It was a nice sound. Like waves lapping at the sandy Californian shore.

"Excuse me for a moment."

I scanned the room properly in his absence. A couple in their early seventies sat watching the pianist intently with the fire softly flickering behind them. An elegant woman sat at the bar sipping from a champagne flute. Was she waiting for her arrangement or was she a business traveler eager to get out of her room?

Mark came back and took my purse confidently from the chair, opening it with the surety that only a married man could.

He swiftly placed an envelope in it, snapped it shut in under 23 seconds and sat a little closer this time. His efficiency combined with how much easier this money would make my life was terribly endearing and I felt a tingle of appreciation surge through my underwear, grateful he'd sat closer.

"What do you like to do?"

"Let's go upstairs, I'll show you."

"I mean when you're not here."

I felt myself blush.

"I surf, badly, but I surf. I uh, like to cook. I'm going to culinary school on weekends."

In truth, the majority of time was spent changing diapers and laundering clothes Sampson had spit up on, but discussion of my son was off limits. Maybe because motherhood didn't feel sexy and the bulk of my culinary skills were spent blending baby food, but also because my love for my squishy-faced, toothless son had to remain tucked away in the most sanctified ventricles of my heart and separate from this.

"Do you want to open your own restaurant?"

"More of a bed and breakfast type of thing. A magnificent ocean front guest house where honeymooners might come to stay for the week and be catered to like royalty."

"You like to take care of people."

"I guess."

"That's a beautiful trait in today's narcissistic world."

We listened to the piano for a song or two, mesmerized by its loveliness.

He reached for my hand. "I have to go. Would you be willing to see me again?"

What? Leaving? But we hadn't even...what the hell?!

"I would."

"I'll message you."

I nodded trying to hide my disappointment behind a smile and then got up, maybe a little too quickly. "Goodnight."

I walked out, swinging my hips in hopes he was watching. I tried to think of an imaginary reason I might be leaving without my husband. Going to pick up my ring from being cleaned perhaps. At this hour the bellman would wonder? Sure, it's Los Angeles, everything is 24-7.

*****

Standing at the sink, I rinse the nipples of the formula I've recently switched to. My breasts have finally dried up and shrunk back to more or less their original proportions. I worked hard to get my body back in shape, but the memory of the past year would always be with it. No amount of Pilates would remove the trauma of what I knew my body was capable of. The physical horrors that appeared one after another seemed like they would never end. *Oh, look my shoes don't fit anymore, my vagina is turning the color of an eggplant and is that hair on my knuckles?*

Joe left and I wasn't surprised. What did surprise me was how little I cared. I wish I could care that little about my phone dinging.

It was possible I'd never hear from Mark again. Maybe he didn't fuck me last time because he didn't want to. That's what I was there for after all. I mean, he had a wife for company, right?

The baby monitor brought me back to reality as my boy softly spoke his poetic non-words.

I wasn't mad at Joe for leaving. I was too soft for anger, too in love with my baby. It was vastly different than anything I'd ever felt. It wasn't even a feeling so much as a ubiquitous light coloring everything in my life. Sampson was the clearing in the forest *and* the beam of sunlight that shone through. I thought about him like he was a crush. What was he thinking? Was his love as deep as mine? What would his voice be like? At barely a year old, he was still a mystery to be unraveled and I could not wait.

Making money for my love so he could sleep on a lamb skin or we could go to Mommy and Me swim class and I could buy all organic ingredients to put in the most expensive blender was something that worried me in the first weeks after Joe left. I quit my job at the health food store in my seventh month and relied on Joe from then on because he'd assured me I could, but he broke his word and that was that.

I picked my boy up from his crib, more for me than for him. He would've been content to lay uttering sweet nothings for hours. It was as though crying never occurred to him. He never had reason to.

We sat on the couch, him lying in my lap kicking his strong little legs, fists submerged in his drool-filled mouth. More teeth would be coming soon and then maybe he'd have something to cry about. If I'd have been able to have sharp little teeth piercing my gums instead, I would have.

And then, it happened. My phone's ding cut the peace like Sampson's teeth soon would, and it was a number I recognized even before seeing the name. Maybe one day I would memorize it.

"What are you doing Thursday?" the screen said.

Should I wait to answer, I wondered? Were there rules to this or was it much more straight forward than that?

I'd get Mrs. Hill's niece to come over. I'd tell her I had another date and she would be happy for me.

I left that evening with a bounce in my step, in spite of the uncomfortable shoes. As I parked in what was now my usual spot, I smiled thinking that this was our third date; traditionally the one in which a relationship is consummated. We'd fast tracked that though.

The doorman recognized me and said hello in a professional but friendly tone. What did he think I was doing here and did he care?

Mark's body visibly relaxed when he saw me and it made me feel like we were old friends, but still sexy new friends too.

His lips brushed within a millimeter of mine as we hugged and the warmth of his breath leaked delicately from within reminding me he was alive just like me.

We only had one drink before heading to the elevators. He reached for my hand once we were inside, bolder now, not caring about the bellman who stared at the doors. His fingers danced flirtatiously with mine and when we got to our floor he stepped ahead confidently leading the way to an equally hip, but entirely different room.

I followed him in, exhilarated with each step.

He strode across the room and opened the sliding door, then stepped out as if a magnet to the shore. I joined him and we stood quietly, listening to the sound of the waves for nearly a minute before he reached up and cupped the nape of my neck, holding me close to his face looking at me inch by inch. I closed my eyes, comfortable with this intimacy before he kissed me hard and deep, penetrating my mouth with his soft tongue.

He ran his fingers through my hair, and then grabbed a handful of it, turning me around to face the ocean. I stretched and arched my back, thirsting for him impatiently.

"Do you know how sexy you are?"

I turned to look at him. "Am I?" I asked coyly.

"I've been thinking about you."

"What have you been thinking?"

"About your skin, how soft it is. How I couldn't wait to touch it again."

He reached up under my dress to my inner thigh and brushed it with his fingers, delicately at first, but then with an unmistakable desire. "Shall we go inside?"

"I can't wait that long."

I turned and he lifted me onto the railing, then knelt before me, taking me in his mouth urgently, but with finesse, as the succulents in the planter behind us looked on. I came quickly, without hesitation because there was no performance required of my genitalia. My softening lent itself to more intense pleasure unlike a man's.

"Are you comfortable?" he asked.

I nodded and smiled. A single man would not think to ask that. "Can I get you anything?"

"Liiiike...?"

"A foot rub? A pillow for that beautiful ass of yours?"

I shook my head as my eyes dropped down to his zipper.

"Is this what you want?" he asked, grabbing his hard cock sideways, reminding me of its girth.

He fucked me softly at first while I exhaled and let him deeper inside. I wrapped my legs around his waist and unbuttoned his shirt, eager for his skin on mine. He had soft brown hair covering his chest and abdomen and I thanked God for my heterosexuality.

When I felt the throb of his upcoming climax, I took him in my mouth and gulped his salty sweet cum. I thought for a moment of Sampson lusting for my breast when he was nursing hungrily and enjoyed the camaraderie for a split second.

I stood, and Mark wrapped his arms firmly around me before kissing me on the forehead, almost paternally, as though he were proud of me. I heard myself giggle.

"I can't stay."

"Okay."

"You can though. Why don't you go mess up the bed? Make housekeeping work for their money."

Money. The word hung in the air for a moment before he took out his wallet and handed me cash that felt so fresh it must've been come directly from the mint. I didn't count it. Was that the difference between me and a real prostitute?

And he was gone. And I was in a stunningly beautiful suite, alone.

I walked through the rooms, marveling at the decor. I thought about stealing towels or the beautiful blown glass bowl that sat elegantly on the entrance table, but the embarrassment of being caught made me blush.

I took a long bath with so many bubbles they rose a full foot above the edge of the tub. I ran my hands over my naked body. Gently, deliberating on places that hadn't felt like my own since before Sampson. I lifted my legs and looked at them. I wiggled my toes and held onto my wrists individually, feeling flesh and bone underneath and the weight of being human.

At least an hour later I got out and stepped into easily the plushest robe I've ever felt. It was long enough to cover my ankles entirely and I felt like a woman of considerable means.

I flopped on the bed and rolled over and back again thinking about the housekeepers. Should I leave a note saying there was no need to change the sheets? I had been a chambermaid as a teenager and would've appreciated that.

I could've stayed. I could've asked Mrs. Hill's niece to spend the night, but this was the land of make believe. I didn't want to get lost here.

Uzair and the Bear

I sit in my tiny home moisturizing my elbows by candle light because I have committed to youthful elbow skin and to solar power, both of which can be sparse at this time of year.

It's not a palace, but I do love my little house. It makes me feel practical and economical but also magical with all of its hidden compartments and everything having dual purposes. The kitchen counter pulls out into a dining table and the stairs double as chairs with just a change in their first two letters. My bed folds up into a couch and the television screen pulls down from the ceiling where it remains discreetly tucked away for the hours I like to pretend I'm truly living off the grid.

The front door is a mix of branches and twigs, woven together and stained so that a neighboring hobbit would feel right at home coming by to borrow a cup of sugar. A cup of sugar would be all the sugar I have room for incidentally, but I'd give it to him because think of how novel it would be to have a hobbit come knocking at your door.

I am fully self-sufficient—a universe of one, and probably appearing like I don't give a good goddamn. Maybe that's true. Maybe I gave up hope when Allen died and left me to grieve through the last of my youth.

Pneumonia—it sounded like such an olden day affliction, but that's what did it. He never recovered from Annapurna. As many times as I told him to go to the doctor he wouldn't, so we kept traveling hoping that the air or sunshine of our next destination was all he needed. Eventually it was too late for doctors and I had to leave him in a hole in the ground drowned in the fluid of his own lungs, stubbornly mistaken about not being ill. For once I hated being right.

The sadness I felt when Allen was no longer was incalculable. It was messier than grief, much less dignified. Grief seemed to imply I wore navy blue pant suits during that time and didn't look up from thick Russian novels, while dining on lukewarm broth through barely parted lips. A widow grieved, but what I did was more what you'd expect from a seriously deranged homeless person.

On Wednesday I had to switch dentists because I called the receptionist an incompetent twat for misspelling my name in spite of my being a patient there for nine and a half years.

On Friday, tired of my meager selection of stale BBQ corn nuts and neon yellow margarine, I went to the grocery store. I wandered the aisles and picked up items that were once familiar but looked alien now. When I snatched a carton of eggs from the painfully slow cashier and they smashed on the tile floor, I was escorted out by security.

I lost the ten pounds I'd been trying to for ten years and then I lost twenty or thirty more and I finally looked as bad as I felt. My clothes hung off of me like a holocaust victim and my nose protruded with a vengeance amid the lack of facial fat that once made it blend in.

Nights were awful. After about 4 days, when the shock wore off and I realized this was actually happening, that I was a *widow*, like for *real*, I cried so hard I gagged as though I might throw up, but as far as I know grief vomiting only happens in movies.

No amount of bargaining or money could undo the truth. Allen's miraculous recovery was no longer worth praying for, even if I had believed in prayer and the lack of control I felt produced ungodly amounts of snot and demonic sounding wails.

I cried like a banshee for about two weeks. I thought about blowing my head off or jumping off a bridge, but I couldn't get it together long enough to deal with the logistics of that.

Friends came by and brought cans of soup and frozen pies, since we were modern folk and no one knew how to make casseroles anymore. My half-sister and her husband sent a card, but we'd never been close and my dad called a few times, but he didn't know what to say and I ended up comforting him, so I stopped answering after a while and I guess he assumed I was fine.

Death discombobulates people because we need to believe on some level that our loved ones are immune to mortality. Foresight to the pain of loss is unbearable, so we get twitchy and say things like, "I can't imagine" but what we *mean* is, I don't want to imagine and you're making that really hard. Please get away from me. Oh, but here's some food so I feel less guilty.

Three years later, my counsellor tried to insist I date, but the idea of making polite conversation with strangers only deepened my longing for my dead husband, so I stopped seeing her. To say I craved a Tuesday night on the couch with Allen cooking, reggae music playing and a neglected book beside me was the understatement of all understatements. Allen was no longer the husband who offered familiarity and solace; he'd morphed into a phantom limb as I groped the dirt trying to pick my heart up without him.

Eventually, I had no fight left in me and instincts suggested flight.

The city, with its vacant crowds and relentless noise no longer appealed to me and I thought about a country home. The irony was that Allen had always wanted us to move the country and I was adamantly opposed, but it made sense now.

I liked the idea of a small place. Just mine for this new chapter of my life that would also be just mine. Maybe if it were itsy-bitsy, it would feel less Allenless and maybe downsizing would eliminate the space I'd kept for self-pity.

I sold our apartment in three days and purchased a small piece of land with a creek and a pear tree about an hour south. It happened fast enough that the angry, rail thin, sob-a-holic I'd become barely noticed until I was at the hardware store for the 18th time and had a sink, tiles and wood flooring as well as what one might call friendship with Herbie, Dave and Pablo who worked there. I looked forward to our easy conversations about lumber and staining and how to install lighting fixtures without getting electrocuted. They never asked me personal questions and that was ideal, so when Herbie offered me a job, I said yes. I didn't need the $15.75 an hour since Allen's insurance plan had left me in good shape, but the companionship and daily routine was very welcome.

Settling into my new life was made easier by the new surroundings. Day-by-day being alone became my new normal and I was no longer a gaping wound. I was able to get through the basics. I went to work, I came home, ate and slept, and though joy was not in my repertoire, I no longer assaulted egg cartons.

I learned about caulking, insulation, different types of nails and their uses and my mind was filled with practicality instead of connection to other humans, until one day a doleful brown-eyed man came in asking for a job. His shoulders hung forward slightly, but his face was earnest and he had beautiful hands. I hired him on the spot in spite of not having the authority to do so.

His name was Uzair.

"What does your name mean?" I asked him one day when we were walking out, he to the bus stop and me to my car.

"Helpful," he smiled, as if that were the best thing in the world to be.

"Do you want a ride home?"

"That would be helpful, yes, thank you."

I smiled at his sweet joke and we formed an instantaneous friendship, as if we'd known each other for 400 years.

"What do you do when you're not working, Uzair?" I asked him one afternoon.

"I am studying life. Learning how I can help people become better people."

"Psychology?" I asked.

He shrugged, without commitment and I dropped it, not wanting to pry.

"Do you think we are born into our names or we become them subconsciously?" he asked pensively.

"My name means bear, so if that's the case, I'm in trouble."

He grinned.

"Ursula the bear. Not as good as yours." I felt embarrassed for a moment, cursing my parents for not naming me something feminine and sweet like Ella or Chantal rather than a lumbering old bear that slept for six months of the year snoring the whole time and living off body fat.

He was looking at his phone now, probably scrolling dating apps for an Ella or Chantal.

"Ah, here we go," he said, "this makes sense. Bears symbolize courage, physical strength and leadership. They are good omens and convey authority according to the Natives."

"Do you see me as an authority figure?"

"Yes!"

"Why?"

"The way you carry yourself; confidently, like you can take care of things."

"I'm tired of taking care of myself."

"Can I help?" He reached for my hand and gave it a gentle squeeze. I felt my heart fuse together a centimeter or two.

"Do you want to come over and listen to records?" I asked.

His eyes got wide.

"You know...records? They came before tapes, which is what came before CDs, which is what came before Napster and iTunes and Spotify, and well, I don't know what comes after that."

"I know what records are; I'd love to! That'd be cool."

Cute. Enthusiasm. Does that fade for everyone or just sad old widows?

We started hanging out a lot. I got acquainted with his face, his voice, and the way his mouth moved when he ate. We danced on my patio and sang loudly into the night air alongside the crickets and slowly, without announcing itself, happiness crept in.

I didn't acknowledge my romantic feelings for him until his soft, pillowy lips met mine with the bravado of youth, sprinkled with the shyness of every good first kiss. It was best that the feelings crept in because I might have fled in guilt or fear or just because that's what a bear does when she feels like she could get trapped.

About three months in, we were laying on our backs on a blanket spread out under the stars when I had to pee. It was most inconvenient. Practical things like piss have no place in the first 3-6 months of a love affair.

Neither did the darkness I felt in him as strongly as the urine pushing the walls of my bladder.

I ran off into the bushes, not wanting to bother fumbling for light switches or taking off my shoes.

As I squatted, I could see the whites of his eyes watching me and I liked feeling seen again.

The rain came, then the snow, and by Spring Uzair opened himself to me like the petals of a peony. He told me of swimming in a salt water lake and of the pomegranate wine his father would brew that made him a town hero due to the scarcity of alcohol in Maragheh.

He'd come to study architecture and I thought of how helpful it would have been to consult with him instead of the countless YouTube videos when I was building my house if time had no meaning and now was then.

I told him about the time my mom went to her sister's for the weekend and never came back. That she had long curly auburn hair and how I could never understand why mine was blonde and straight. That was the same week Rebecca Munroe had knocked the wind out of me with one punch to the stomach, after I'd taken my scissors to her favorite doll's face. I didn't want her cheeks to be so rosy, so I tried to scratch them off. I denied it and she got sent to the principal's office while everyone huddled around me coddling with concern.

I didn't talk about Allen. That was between me and Allen.

One night as we lay in bed listening to a thunder storm that had threatened for three days, Uzair confused and then intrigued me with a question.

"Would you hurt me?"

I rolled over and took his face in my hands.

"No, kitten. I respect you. I care about you."

"That's not what I mean."

"We've all been hurt. It's okay."

"I'm not the man you think I am."

"Huh?"

"Never mind."

"No, tell me."

"I didn't leave Iran to come to college."

"Goodness is relative. Morals are objective. Don't buy into that crap."

The clouds overhead hung low, full to capacity and backlit by the moon.

"I got my girlfriend pregnant. She wasn't a girlfriend though, not in the American way. She was a neighbor that had eyes for me and when I was 15, I succumbed."

The sky opened up and rain began, drip, drop, dripping from the sky.

"I didn't want to marry her, particularly because I could see how excited she was that she had finally got her way and her impoverished confidence turned my stomach. I liked the way her body felt in the dark behind the rock pile, but that was all. I didn't care for talking to her; she was simple, one-dimensional. She would meet me, I would have relations with her and I would leave feeling lighter in my step, less burdened by my responsibilities and like there was more to me than the responsible eldest son.

The pregnancy emboldened her and made me dislike her even more. She told her sisters that I was to be her husband. She told them that I was a prince and that she would be my princess and I hated her juvenile lies, so I stole from my father and mother and I hitched a ride to Tehran. I haven't talked to anyone from there since."

The sound of raindrops was forceful now; it sounded exquisite on the tiny tin roof as I tried to process my lover's hostility toward a woman I'd never meet.

"What was her name?"

"They stoned her to death in the square after her family fled in shame. They probably used the same rocks she used to spread her legs behind."

"What was her name?"

His voice cracked. "Roshan."

I sat up and walked around the bed to his side. I felt strength in my bones as I hoisted him up like a loose bag of dirt. He stood with his head bowed as I closed my fist, punching him hard in the chest.

He winced, but stayed put and I liked the way the resistance to my rage felt.

Exhilarated by his steady stance, I took the heel of my hand and jammed it into his forehead as hard as I could, feeling my power like I hadn't in years. He stumbled and fell back on the bed, looking a little surprised. I mounted him, pinning his arms and meeting his eyes with mine. We stared at each other a moment, swimming in the depths of our pain.

"Go on," he said.

I reached for a handful of his thick black hair, so soft that it was hard to keep my grip, and pulled him up to a sitting position.

I took him by the shoulders and shook him like he was a large bottle of Kombucha. When I tired of that, he scooted back a little and I slammed him in the headboard, his neck lolling dizzily.

While he got his equilibrium back, I tore my fingernails down his arms and then twisted his skin back and forth, smiling as he cried out in pain.

I pinched the inside of his thighs and gave his penis a forceful yank.

"Owww!"

"That's from Roshan, you shit! How could you leave her?! She needed you!"

He hung his head.

"How dare you! How dare you leave her!"

"I'm sorry."

"You left!"

"I won't leave."

I slapped him hard across the face.

"Say it again."

"I won't leave you."

He pulled me down on top of him and the fallacy that I was in physical control evaporated.

He held me tightly as I burrowed into his neck and inhaled the scent of our tears.

And I Was Like November

Like the funk of asparagus ruminating in urine long after its appearance on the plate, the acrimony of our relationship still sat heavy on my heart.

I'd had others since. I hoped their hairless scrota and selfish intentions might clear him from my energy field like a slutty Reiki remedy. Instead it made him feel further away and my voice more brittle. He changed his profile pic, his arm slung over the shoulder of a simpleton wearing beige Spanx as a dress and tattoos that screamed: 'I'm basic, but I'm fooling everyone!' His face was hard to read, even for me who thought I knew his every expression after three years. I'd never seen that shirt either, so maybe he was altogether different. Maybe now he could communicate with complete sentences that articulated his feelings instead of running off to the city for boy's nights with that idiot he called friend.

I called the idiot once when Daniel was pulling away. I wanted to casually inquire, figuring as an actor he'd be sensitive to feelings of inadequacy, but he was not sensitive and crying and begging a near stranger not to betray what a mess you are is not casual.

It was always the same. I needed more than he could give. He needed less than I could hold back. I'd bring him lunch at the studio or moisturize his cuticles and he would say he didn't deserve me, which made me want to prove his worth to him as a substitute for my own. He hugged me so hard then and everything felt safe with my face pressed into his T-shirt, his familiar scent lulling my fears into submission. Then I'd stay. I wanted another hit of affection. Only want wasn't a strong enough word. I wanted it like a 3-year-old child left in a gas station bathroom wants her mom to pick her up instead of the needle.

That day at Chevron was the final time she left me. I didn't see her for four years from then, during which time custody was given to my aunt and uncle after bouncing between foster homes. When they filled out the paperwork, they said they were Christian. That meant on Sundays my bushy-browed aunt pressed my feet into uncomfortable patent leather shoes and I'd take communion. They said the dry wafer with a cross on it was the body of Christ, but I was never clear why I'd want to put that in my mouth. Did someone confuse cannibalism with Catholicism?

When I was seven, they took me to see my Mommy. She joked with the prison guard as she walked up in her grey sweatsuit the same as the other ladies I saw throughout the yard. It was nice to be comfortable in jail, I guessed. She gave me a bible. Inside it said, 'God Bless You, pumpkin' in her bubble handwriting as small as she was tall. Day after day I flipped through its pages the texture of my dad's rolling papers, trying to make sense of the tiny scripture with no luck. I hoped that somewhere she would've written another message. Something that actually meant something like, 'Meet me behind the cherry tree at 8 on Tuesday, let's blow this joint,' but all I could find were psalms and smite and the word Lord with a capital L. She gave it to me because it was the only thing she had to give and because she wouldn't miss it. Unlike her sister, she didn't pretend to be something she wasn't.

"How's my #1 daughter?," she asked in her throaty voice.

She picked me up and swung me so high that my grandma winced with concern. I wished she would toss me high enough to fly and she would fly too and we would fly far, far away from all this nonsense.

I was at her bedside while she died for five days. It was the most time I'd spent with her in as long as I could remember. Beads of sweat sat on her brow and in the nooks of her neck. I ran the wash cloth under cold water and lay it on her forehead until it was too hot to touch and then repeat. The doctor said not to kiss her on the lips because her saliva was toxic. I hoped she didn't hear him because that wouldn't make me feel very good if I were her.

Did this new skank love him gently enough not to smother him? When that dry blue hair touched his naked chest, did he wish she took the time to condition that I did? She probably didn't care; she was the kind of girl that didn't need his approval. That was probably what he liked best about her. She wasn't me with all my complicated wounds.

He'd once told me that the bullying got so bad, he'd wake up in the morning with his eyes glued shut by the saltiness of his tears. Did she know about that or did he keep it light because that is what he wanted all along? To forget the darkness. And I was like November, only light for a few hours a day or sometimes not at all when the clouds rolled in.